Walking the Thames River Path

One Woman's Solo Journey
of Adventure and Self-Discovery

Joyce Mackie

DISCLAIMER

Disclaimer and Terms of Use: Effort has been made to ensure that the information in this book is accurate and complete, however, the author and the publisher do not warrant the accuracy of the information, text, and graphics contained within the book due to the rapidly changing nature of science, research, known and unknown facts, and the Internet.

MAP OF THE UNITED KINGDOM

THAMES RIVER (Blue)
THE THAMES PATH (Red)

Courtesy of Google Maps and Britain Express

Table of Contents

ABOUT THE THAMES RIVER

The 215-mile-long Thames River has numerous loops and twenty major tributaries. Many rivers flow into it. It begins as a trickle from an underground spring in the Cotswolds, southwest of London, and gradually becomes a stream, slowly widening and deepening as it passes through the Chilterns. It winds its way through open fields, villages, and vast expanses of meadows, over weirs and under bridges, through locks, past villages, parks and gardens, fine buildings, castles and warehouse, along docks, and finally flows out to meet the North Sea. On its journey to the sea, it becomes a fast-moving, ever-changing river full of life--birds, boats, barges, fishers, and pleasure-seekers.

For centuries, the Thames has been a subject of natural beauty for artists and writers.   One never knows what sights await around the next bend--breath-taking vistas of the river and meadows and hills, locks and villages and castles, bridges and country estates.

In the minds of some, the Thames represents England. It is one of the most historic rivers anywhere. Much of the history of England is rooted in, and along, the Thames River. From prehistoric times, the river has been an important part of English history. Tools, weapons, and animal and human bones from around 3500 BC have been dug up on the banks of the Thames. Remains of forts and huts from Roman and Saxon settlements have been found there.

The Thames, a central figure in English life, has played many roles. It is a river of contrasts and contradictions. It has been home to convicts in the prison hulks (ships where convicts and other outcasts of society were held under terrible conditions) of the late 1700s to early 1800s, and in contrast, royalty has lived along its banks for centuries.

In its earliest years, people drank its pure waters. By the 1800s, however, the Thames had become a sewer of disease, pollution and putrid odors. It was many years before significant steps were taken to revive the river.

Many have found pleasure and sport on the Thames--boating, fishing, and rowing; for others, it has been a working river--a river of trade and commerce.

It can be a quiet, placid river, or powerful, fast-moving and stormy. There have been many serious floods. In 1953, a surge tide drowned fifty-eight people on Convey Island. Between 1620 and 1814, the river froze over twenty-three times. Some years, shops and entertainment were set up on ice that was up to eighteen inches thick--virtual cities where crowds thronged to experience the novelty. While this was an enjoyable experience for some, it was disastrous for others. Those whose livelihood depended on a flowing river--dock and wharf workers, and fishermen, suffered. In the worst year, 1434-35, when the river was immobile for two and a half months, some starved, froze or died from the cold.

The Thames was an important trade route around 50 AD. The Romans developed the Port of London into a major center for ship-building and commerce. But the tidal swift currents that made London a great port caused disastrous flooding in later years.

Throughout history, rivers have been considered sacred. Churches have been built on the banks of the Thames; the dead have been buried there; and baptisms, healings, weddings and rituals have been performed on its waters. But while the Thames has been a witness to much celebration and revelry, it has also been at the center of tragedy, punishment and death. For example, in 1879, the Princess Alice, a pleasure paddle steamer carrying 1000 passengers, collided with a steam collier and sank. Most on board were drowned.

The Thames is the subject of many legends and superstitions. Some believed it was the home of dangerous gods that must be appeased. For others, the river represents the dark unknown. The Thames itself is impartial. During World War Two, when it was carrying ships and supplies to London, it was also serving as a guideline for the German fighter planes finding their way to London.

The Thames River has been an enduring presence throughout the calm and the turbulent history of England--not always predictable, but always intriguing.

INTRODUCTION

The Thames River Path first caught my imagination some years ago, when I read an article about the walk along the hundred-mile towpath that had been used by men and horses to pull river barges up the river in the late eighteenth century. This was before the advent of locks. (By contrast, there are now forty-five locks on the river.)

The article's description of the picturesque countryside and the charming inns and cottages along the way entranced me. When the article was written, the guided tour of the towpath was divided into segments of ten miles of walking per day. At that time, I didn't have the means to go to England, and I wasn't sure I could walk that far every day. I loved the idea but filed the article away, and it soon became a dim memory. That is, until, in 2006, I attended a travel presentation on another walk that a couple had taken across England from east to west. That walk sounded very strenuous, difficult, and demanding in every way. I had no desire to replicate their trip, but it did reawaken within me memories of the Thames towpath that I had read about years earlier.

When I went home that evening, I pulled out the article and read it with renewed interest. Sparked by the presentation I had seen, I began research on the Thames towpath. I discovered that the towpath was now part of a National Trail that had been extended to follow the river from its source to its estuary at London, a distance of 184 miles. The English

Ramblers' Association had published an official guidebook written by David Sharp, which according to the book review, gave quite detailed directions for following the Path each day. It divided the route into fifteen sections, one for each day, and described points of interest along the way.

Now I was really intrigued. However, a big question remained in my mind: Could I walk ten to fifteen miles every day for fifteen consecutive days, as outlined in the guidebook? I was sixty-nine years old, and though I walked regularly, I had never walked more than five miles at a stretch, and certainly not carrying a backpack of over ten pounds. However, I loved walking and adventure, and I welcomed the mental, physical and spiritual challenges. In addition, I wanted to see England, especially the countryside.

Eventually, my desire to do the walk overcame my doubts and misgivings. My next step, I thought, would be easy – just find out when the next hiking or tour group was going and sign up. No luck. It seemed that no one was walking the Path. Okay, I thought, I'll find someone to go with me, even a friend of a friend. I asked friends and family. I asked in outdoor stores. No one had even heard of the Thames Path.

Finally, the realization came to me that, if I wanted to do this walk, I would have to go alone. At first, I dismissed the idea; it filled me with apprehension. But the images of the Thames stuck in the back of my mind and kept pulling at me, until at last, I gave the idea full consideration. Over a couple of weeks, I did more research. The guidebook that I needed would have to be ordered from England. Once I had the guidebook, I would have a better idea of what I would be up against if I went on my own. When the book arrived, I studied it and became so excited with the possibilities, the adventure, and the sights I would see, that I made up my mind to do the walk.

The guidebook outlined where to travel each day and gave detailed directions on what landmarks and geographical features to look for. Another book provided valuable information on places to stay overnight.

So the walk itself was all laid out for me. Now, how would I train for it? What would I take with me? When would I go?

I was faced with a huge learning curve. I didn't know how to train or how long it would take me to train. I didn't know what gear I would need. I wasn't sure I could walk an average of fifteen miles per day carrying a backpack containing all my food, water, clothes, reading and writing materials, personal items, utensils, and rain gear.

I sought advice from everyone who knew anything about walking and backpacking long distances. I bought the best gear I could afford. I worked out a training schedule that would allow me to gradually increase the distance walked and the weight I carried. I researched what to eat and when. I learned the proper way to put on a backpack. (The friend who showed me was appalled when she saw how I had been doing this.)

I started training in January, with plans to begin the walk the following September. I would have eight months to prepare my body and mind for success. I set goals for each week, gradually increasing my mileage and my load. I didn't achieve my goal every week, but I learned that a missed week need not dictate the next week's results.

There were days when it was too icy to walk outdoors and days when it was rainy and windy. The fear that I might not be ready in time drove me out of the house to walk, even when I would much rather have stayed indoors.

Another incentive to train was the prospect of exploring new places and seeing new things right where I lived. Sometimes I walked along the waterfront and through residential districts where I had never been before. In the Victoria, BC area, there were two long hiking trails that wound through fields and forests, and skirted highways and busy streets. Always, there was that sense of accomplishment when I walked farther and longer than before. Gradually, as I gained endurance, I became more confident of my ultimate success. It was encouraging to know that I usually recovered quickly from the previous day's training.

It began to take up a lot of my time. My average walking speed was one mile in sixteen minutes. Therefore, to walk fifteen miles, I needed four hours of practice time.

Also, I was spending a lot of time searching for the best gear I could afford. (See Appendix for a list.) Later I was to discover that all the time and money I had spent on gear paid off in comfort and convenience. I stayed warm and dry in the worst weather. The water bladder I carried, which fit into the inside of my backpack, gave me an easily accessible supply of water. It had a tube that fed through a hole in the pack and over my shoulder. I could take sips of water throughout the day whenever I needed it, rather than stopping to gulp huge amounts when I was really thirsty.

A friend who is a seasoned hiker advised me on how to get my backpack weight down to a minimum. As I packed, I scrutinized every item I set out to take with me. Did I really need it? Could I put it in a smaller, lighter container? I even removed a pair of unnecessary straps from my backpack and shortened others to reduce the weight. My friend was impressed that I was able to get it down to fourteen pounds including the pack and water.

As it turned out, I had prepared well, for I had everything I needed on the trip, and nothing that I should have left at home. I didn't take binoculars because of the extra weight. I opted not to take a camera, because stopping on the trail to grab my camera, take a photo, then re-stash my camera would slow me down. Also I have found that if I am concentrating on taking a photo, I often miss something of the moment. I didn't take a cell phone either. They were relatively new, and I had no idea how they would work out in England. After my trip, I learned that there was a company in England that sold phones that could be used when traveling, then returned to the company for a refund. I did take a GPS, but I never mastered its use.

The biggest preparation was mental – trusting that God would be with me and guide the way. I believed that my training would prepare me physically and the guidebooks would direct me to where I needed to go on the Path and where to find lodging. Did I know I could do it? No. What I did know was that I could lean on God for help. I set out on the trip fairly confident about my success, but it wasn't until I finished the first day of walking that I had evidence I could do it.

My family was very supportive of my plans. They thought, as I did, that the Thames Path was a wide, well-travelled trail with many people walking in both directions. Little did we know it was not at all like that. One friend around my age voiced her concern. She tactfully asked if the walk might be too much at my age, reminding me that I wasn't as young as I used to be. My reply was that it had nothing to do with age, but with mental and physical fitness.

I had basically two concerns. First, the amount of weight I would be carrying. I hadn't trained with fourteen pounds. Would I find it too much? Second, I was apprehensive about finding my way around London. In this huge city, how would I find a place to stay? What would it be like getting from one place to another?

This book is about my experience walking along the Thames River Path in England. Come with me and discover what it is like to see the Thames grow from its barely visible beginnings in a meadow under a tree to its mighty exit, miles away at the sea. I invite you to walk along with me as we observe life on the river today and get a glimpse of its past. There are wondrous sights along the way, and you will be amazed at what awaits around the next bend.

Come with me and share my hardships and challenges, my mishaps and victories, my disappointments and moments of exhilaration. My hope is that you will be inspired, entertained and informed. I gained immeasurably from my experience; and I trust that you will gain from reading about it.

For those of you who like to walk and love adventure with a personal challenge, you will be encouraged to follow the Path, to go solo, or to try something else that you've always wanted to do.

BATH, LACOCK, STONEHENGE

Before starting on the Thames Path, I took a couple of days to visit Bath and Stonehenge, situated almost directly south of the Thames River source.

As the English countryside slid past my train window on the way to Bath, I delighted in every eyeful. It was as I had pictured it: green and harvested fields divided by rows of hedges, farmhouses dotting the landscape, cottages clustered in quaint villages. I had never been to England, or any other European country; everything was new to me. From Gatwick to Bath, I drank it all in, amazed and awed by the charm of the countryside.

I learned that England has a maritime climate--limited seasonal temperature ranges and generally moderate rainfall throughout the year. During my visit to England, at the end of September and early October, the fall weather was unseasonably warm after a cold, rainy summer. People were basking in the unusually warm, sunny days.

Stepping out of the train station at Bath, I stood there, speechless at the sight. I couldn't believe my eyes! This was like no other town I had ever seen. It was like something from another time, or from a movie set. The golden-colored stone buildings, situated on both sides of a central street, were old and so different and quaint to me, and none seemed immediately recognizable as to their function. I tried to take it all in.

Then I realized I had absolutely no idea where to go--so I plunged straight ahead, wide-eyed, as I tried to get my mind to focus. At the first intersection, I spied a map of the city posted on a billboard. Aha, I thought, there must be others who feel as lost as I do when they arrive here. I located the tourist information bureau on the map, and set out to find it.

After some walking, I needed to find a washroom. Having only a vague idea of where I was at this point, I asked a man where the nearest bathroom was. (In Canada, we use the terms washroom, bathroom, and restroom rather interchangeably.) He stared at me with a mix of disbelief, bewilderment, and annoyance. I repeated the question, this time asking for a washroom. And then I knew why he had looked at me that way. Here I was, standing next to the Baths and asking to use a bathroom! I laughed to myself as I turned and headed in the direction he indicated.

Lo and behold, the washroom was in the Abbey, right next to the Bath Spa. Such splendid architecture! My mouth must have been hanging open at the sight. I had never seen anything like it. But I would have to wait until the next day to explore.

At the tourist bureau, I was delighted to find many useful leaflets. From directions on one, I located Juice Kitchen, and there I downed a smoothie as if my body had been crying out for it. Still thinking of food, I continued walking until I found Harvest, a health food store. I purchased raw food bars and, in the adjoining deli, indulged in quiche and delicious, fresh organic tomatoes.

Now I was ready to look for my B&B (bed and breakfast accommodation). I was grateful for the 'angel' sent to my aid, who even walked part way with me. This kind woman was on her way home across the River Avon on the outskirts of town. Without her assistance, I might have gone far out of my way.

After I left her, I carried on through a section of what would later become Two Tunnels path, a four- mile route for walkers and cyclists, through disused railway tunnels which were converted into paths that officially opened in 2013. One of the dimly lit tunnels is over one mile long and music is played in the middle. This is part of the much-longer scenic Greenway countryside route for cyclists.

My two-night stay in Bath at the luxurious Chiltern House B&B was a belated birthday gift from my son and daughter. Late summer flowers still provided lots of color in the attractive gardens, even though it was now well into fall. My room was small, but nicely furnished. The dining room held eight round dining tables, each with seats for six. At breakfast, I was disappointed to be seated alone (A server had directed me to a seat.), and therefore had no opportunity to converse with the other guests who came and went. I enjoyed the many choices of fresh fruit, cereal, whole wheat toast, butter and marmalade.

The Romans built the city of Bath on one of the then-major roads, Fosse Way. It was intended to be used for recreation, perhaps because of the hot springs there. Around 60 AD, over a period of more than three hundred years, they built a complex of baths and a temple. After the Roman occupation of England ended in the fifth century, the three original baths (one heated from underground springs, one cold, and one for healing) were neglected and eventually lost to floods and silting. In 1878, Roman remains were unearthed and this led to excavation of the first bath spas. A cache of 30,000 silver Roman coins believed to date from the third century was unearthed in Bath in March, 2012.

Over the years, the baths have been modified many times. In 2006, Bath's historic spas were finally revived and restored, and are now available to the public for bathing in the warm, mineral waters.

The next day, I walked around Bath and admired the mostly Georgian-style buildings that harmonized so pleasingly with the landscaping and the natural setting of the surrounding hills. Yes, being in Bath was like being on a movie set. The whole city was so intriguing. Each street offered something different in its layout and in the style and arrangement of its buildings. My tour book directed me to the historic Sally Lunn, an authentic English eating-house famous for Sally Lunn buns, an English favorite. This charming four-story house, one of the oldest in Bath, had flowers spilling out of the window boxes at every window.

Bath Abbey (Abbey Church of St. Peter and St. Paul) is spectacular. With pinnacles, columns of honey-gold stone, ladders of angels on the west front, and stained glass windows, it is surely the most impressive-looking building in Bath. The church has undergone many changes. One example is the splendid stone fan vaulting over the nave which replaced a wooden ceiling in 1864-74. The present

Abbey was begun in 1499, following the two other churches which had occupied the site: a monastery stood there in Anglo-Saxon times, and later a massive Norman cathedral.

There was much more to the Baths than I had thought. The spa was large, with many pools. I crawled through the underground areas to see it all. Then, wandering around on my own, I picked up snatches of conversation from guides on tours. It was a fascinating place that I would love to have seen in Roman times.

Next to the baths is The Grand Pump Room, a historic building begun in 1789 and finished ten years later. Drinking water could be had here, and it was also a meeting center and restaurant popular with the upper class.

Another major tourist attraction is the Royal Crescent, built 1767-1775, containing some thirty terraced houses. It is a world landmark and considered to be one of the greatest examples of Georgian architecture. One of the houses has been turned into the Royal Crescent Hotel, and another is now the History of Georgian Living Museum.

In the eighteenth century, Bath was a very popular recreational center for the well-to-do; later, it became a cultural center as well, and now it is a major tourism center. Bath has five theaters, many museums, and two universities. It hosts many sporting events and has well-established technology industries. In 1987, the whole city was designated a World Heritage site, with around five thousand listed buildings.

There was so much more to see in Bath. However, I had booked a tour to Stonehenge, which included a stop at Lacock in Wiltshire.

Lacock is a well-preserved village, with houses dating from the fifteenth through the eighteenth century. I was delighted to have an opportunity to see this example of an authentic historic village in southern England. The village was given to the National Trust in 1944 and is now almost entirely owned by it. Lacock was said to have had a population of 160-190 people in 1086, and included two mills and a vineyard. Today, there are five pubs, a teahouse, hall, church, museum, school, store and post office, bakery and eighty-nine houses. Many seek to live in this thriving community, but not everyone is granted accommodation.

Lacock has been used as a film set for Harry Potter films, TV programs and BBC productions including "Pride and Prejudice".

When we arrived in Lacock, the tour driver dropped us off at the George Inn, a local public house dating back to 1361 and on the list of best pubs in England in 2006. It looked as if it had remained unchanged for centuries. The low-beamed ceilings were the same. The rustic fireplace was still in use, but the turnspit dog no longer ran on the treadmill used to turn the spit on which meat was once roasted over the open fire. Atmosphere seeped out of every dark corner. I was fascinated by it. It was so authentic, I was instantly transported in my imagination to a time long ago, when people sat at the same large board tables and ate and drank their ale just as they were doing now.

Tour map in hand, I left through the back door that led into a parking lot. As I stepped into the street lined with neatly laid-out buildings, I noticed that this was no modernized village. Power and telephone lines and TV antennas were hidden underground to preserve the authenticity. There was very little landscaping in the small spaces around the buildings, no expanses of lawns, mostly finely crushed stone.

I peered in at the eighteenth-century lock-up, and checked my map for information on the tithing barn. Apparently, in the Middle Ages, Lacock had rich farmlands and a thriving wool industry. One-tenth of the farmers' produce was stored for the church in tithing barns such as this one, built in the fourteenth century.

One of the churches that tithing may have supported was the parish Church of St. Cyriac, established in the late eleventh century, with only fragments of this early structure remaining. Around 1450, some rebuilding was done. The nearby Abbey was established in 1232.

We left Lacock behind, and drove twenty-four miles to Stonehenge.

Stonehenge, the famous prehistoric remains of huge stones standing in a circular formation, is located on the plains near Amesbury. Archaeological digs over the years have found evidence to indicate that Stonehenge was built sometime between 3000 BC and 2000 BC. How the mammoth bluestones, originating in Wales, were moved to Stonehenge remains a mystery. One theory is that they were moved by glaciers to this area long before they were erected at Stonehenge.

Some believe that Stonehenge was a site of religious significance. Other theories maintain it was a celestial observatory, a healing site, a hunting grounds, or even an alien landing place.

I was somewhat disappointed in Stonehenge. Visitors had to stand far back from the stones; a ditch and a fence separated us from any contact with them. I didn't feel any sense of sacredness, nor did I pick up any energy from them. Mostly, it felt touristy to me. I understand that the site has to be protected from vandals and overzealous sightseers, but in my view, the tourist center with the usual brochures and concession stand detracted from any authentic atmosphere the place may have had. Perhaps my reaction would have been more favorable had there not been crowds of people.

However, when I wandered across the fields, away from the site to some nearby burial mounds, I had a different experience. Casting my eyes across the plains, I could see for miles. As I stood there, alone with the wind on my face, I began to feel a sense of that long-lost era, when people occupied this place; I could feel a connection to the land and the times.

I thoroughly enjoyed the return drive down the back roads between Stonehenge and Bath: the open fields and centuries-old hamlets along the way, the houses joined together and lining the road. The driver/tour guide entertained us with stories about this area and England in general.

There wasn't enough time left in Bath to tour the Jane Austen and the Fashion museums, poke around in shops, or see the

Pulteney Bridge. I needed to buy a phone card, get my train ticket for tomorrow, and phone the hotel in Cricklade to confirm that night's reservation. Before I could do that, I had to find my way around Bath, and figure out how to use the phone--no easy tasks.

That accomplished, I purchased some takeout dinner and walked back to my B&B. After dinner, as I did my laundry, wrote in my journal, showered, and settled into bed, there was one thought predominant in my mind---tomorrow I would begin what I really came for.

DAY 1 ON THE PATH

SOURCE - ASHTON KEYNES

I awoke with great anticipation. This was the day I had come for, had worked for, and now it was to begin. I was ready, but a little apprehensive, trying to stay calm. My plan was to be on the trail by nine, but the incoming train was late arriving in Bath. A newly-retired librarian from Victoria, BC, my hometown, was also anxiously inquiring at the train station as to when the train would arrive, or when another train might be leaving for Kemble station. An impatient half hour or so later, the train came in and soon we alighted in Kemble. Now I was one and a half hours behind my schedule.

I would have to walk upstream from Kemble to reach the source of the Thames, where the Path began, then double back along the Path to Kemble and continue downstream.

I walked through the train station, found the approach road, joined another road that took me along a signed path, across a stile, along a stream, over a footbridge, along the bank of the now-empty Thames, up a broad valley, to the left-hand side of a field, and through a gate to what, if I'd followed the guidebook correctly, was Lyd Well, an ancient spring. I wasn't sure that the little basin with overhanging trees and bushes and a little water that I had passed actually was Lyd Well. There were no Thames Path signs, with the acorn insignia of the National Trails, at this point. I didn't know where I was. Even by my terms, that meant I was lost.

I was soon to discover that, when they call the Thames River Path a "path," it is not to be taken too literally. When I walked the Path (in 2007), it was not actually a physical path that was easily visible. Most of the time, there was no path at all. I had to rely on Thames Path signs posted on gates, trees and, in a few cases, buildings. Sometimes these had disappeared due to weather or other causes. My guidebook was invaluable in giving direction and distinguishable landmarks, but it still wasn't enough. The Path, level except for one wide detour over a steep hill, was maintained by only a few volunteers, insufficient to patrol and maintain the path at regular intervals. Although I depended on the guidebook, it was not always reliable. Terrain changed--a tree that had been identified as a landmark may have blown down, a detour may have been removed, a route may have been altered, or there was no longer a sign where indicated.

It would have been easy to stay on the Path if it had followed the riverbank all the way; however, this was impossible because of vegetation along the river, flooded water meadows, and buildings and land along the river with no right of way.

The big stone Cotswold house mentioned in the guidebook was sitting at the top of the hill in a field across from me, but I couldn't make sense of the directions from there. I tried everything I could think of, but I couldn't find my way.

It was very hot. I was tired. I was dejected. I struggled out of my heavy backpack, sat down, and leaned against a fencepost, without shelter from the hot sun. I couldn't make sense of the guidebook instructions. I was discouraged and frustrated, but not beaten. I prayed, "I don't know where to go. I don't know what to try next. Please help me."

I had an inspiration to go further along a route I had already tried. I kept going, still not sure that I was on the Path. Finally, I recognized some of the landmarks mentioned in the guide. I made my way to Roman Foss Way, a still-travelled ancient major Roman road. Some stone steps, a stile, a cautious road-crossing through traffic, a track through a gate in a long stone wall, a stile, and…. I was lost again. The "faint track marked by a straggly line of trees" was not to be seen.

Time passed with more trial and error, and at last--Hallelujah!--I spied the old ash tree. At its feet there were only some pebbles and a blackened upright stone to mark the spot where one day the trickle of water would again appear from its source underground. The weathered inscription on the stone read, "The Conservators of the River Thames 1857-1974." Victory at last! What a relief!

It had taken me three and a half hours to find this spot, which was only a mile and a half from Kemble. Now I was faced with finding my way back, a sobering thought indeed. I didn't know how I got there. How was I to find my way back? I had made so many turns and backtracked so many times.

I am not good with directions. (Ask my family and friends.) Going back to Kemble should have been easy, but I was now coming from the opposite direction; I would be viewing the way from a different angle and noticing features I hadn't seen earlier.

I can only say (with some pride, I admit) that it didn't take me three and a half hours, to find my way back. By the time I did, however, it was mid-afternoon. I had twelve miles to go before dark if I was to reach Cricklade, my reserved place for the night.

I had still more difficulty following the guidebook directions-- some signs mentioned were no longer there; there had been changes in the Path since the book was published; and parts of the trail were overgrown with grass and shrubs. And where the Thames may have been clearly visible here in the rainy season, now there was at times little or no water, and when there was water, it was hard for me to tell if it was the river or water left standing from recent floods.

Through soggy fields and cow pastures, stinging nettles and brambles, over stiles and footbridges, past picturesque farms, I walked. Stiles were new to me. I had never seen one. As I climbed over the first stile, I smiled and thought about the folktale of the old woman who tried to get her pig to go over the stile so she could get home that night.

Between fields and pastures, there were gates, gates, and more gates, some easy to open, others very tricky. Many different types of latches were used; some gates were tied shut with rope. Some required all my strength to open and close.

I saw a rabbit, an owl, and birds that I didn't know. I talked to cows in the fields and passed by horses and a few sheep. It wasn't unusual for the cattle to be standing on the Path in front of me and not even move as I approached. Having been raised on a farm with cattle, I was at ease around them, and it was comforting to see something familiar. But I was cautious, for when I was a kid, I had been butted down a cactus-dotted lake bank by a steer which suddenly turned on me.

I just kept going, pausing to study my guidebook and decide where to go next to find my way. Finally, I gave up on the guidebook and followed my instincts. At times, there was someone to ask for directions, but most had never heard of the Thames Path. I stopped now and then, never for longer than ten minutes, to rest and eat. Somehow I had the energy to keep going. I became so absorbed in all the wonderful new sights, I often forgot how hot and tired I was.

Such lovely country! I immediately fell in love with the Cotswolds. It was easy to see why it was designated an Area of Outstanding Natural Beauty in 1966. The famous Cotswold stone, found in buildings throughout the area, provided a richness and a sense of stability. The stone varied in color, depending on where the Jurassic limestone was quarried.

There are many sites of scientific interest in the area. Remains of Bronze and Iron Age forts have been found from south of Bath to Stratford-Avon. During the Middle Ages, the prosperous wool trade in the area funded the construction and maintenance of numerous churches, some still to be seen.

Away from the villages, few buildings hide the horizon. There is a sense of freedom and infinity. The wide open spaces of cow pastures and farm fields, where you could hear dogs barking or cows mooing from miles away, reminded me of the Saskatchewan prairies in Canada, where I grew up. The smell of the Cotswolds, a mixture of composting grass, fields and meadows, sweeps across the land and seems to be an integral part of its identity.

But here, unlike my childhood home, there were many bridges crossing meandering streams, as the Thames wove its way through the countryside.

The Path led past some stone cottages at Ewen, my first glimpse of a tiny 'village' on the Thames since leaving Kemble. Ewen has a pub, but no shops. Conscious of the late hour, I paused only a few moments.

Dusk fell. It was almost seven, and I knew I wasn't going to make it to Cricklade, five miles away, before total darkness set in.

The guidebook gave directions to the White Hart Inn in the village of Ashton Keynes, just ahead. I wondered if this was the Inn where I had reserved a room. I thought it unlikely that there would be a White Hart Inn in two villages so close together. Had I confused Cricklade with Ashton Keynes? I remembered debating, when I was planning the trip, whether or not to make my first day shorter and less strenuous by going only as far as Ashton Keynes. Because I couldn't find accommodation there, I had made a reservation in the next village, Cricklade, or so I thought. And as it turned out, I had, indeed, reserved in Cricklade.

The White Hart Inn at Ashton Keynes was fully booked. A very friendly woman on staff told me about a B&B next door. She was doubtful that there would be a room, but suggested I try it. I went out into the darkness and rang the doorbell. The woman who answered the door was hesitant when I asked for a room, but after hearing my story, she thought it over. Then she obligingly gave me a room next to the front door, apparently a room that usually accommodated some hired help. Good. I sighed with relief. I wouldn't have to find my way to Cricklade that night.

I returned to the Inn. The same woman who helped me earlier now went out of her way to provide me with a phone to call the Cricklade Inn, so I could change my reservation to the following night. That taken care of, I was ready to order dinner. They weren't sure what they could provide for a vegetarian meal. We settled on something both on and off the menu. Except for the barely-cooked, hard-to-chew greens, the cooks had made a good attempt. I was grateful for a real, cooked meal. This pub had won an award for "Best Community Pub" in the southwest region in Great Britain. (In 2011, it became collectively owned and run by a number of village residents.)

I dragged myself back to the B&B and managed to secure some time alone in the shared bathroom. I soaked in the tub as long as I thought considerate. It felt so good! As I lay there, I thought over my day. What a day! I hadn't known that I could walk so far for so long, and with a fourteen-pound pack on my back. I had trained with a backpack, of course, but never with a full one, or on such a hot day.

I was pleased that I had been able to meet and pass my tests. I knew I hadn't done it alone. There were times when I simply had to sit down and ask Spirit for help. And help always came. Either I was given inspiration to try this or that or, as on one occasion, people appeared (were sent my way) on the Path, who were able to give me directions.

A part of me was grateful that my first day had been so strenuous and challenging. If I could, on my first day, spend eight and a half hours on the trail in the heat, carrying a full backpack and totally lost at times, with no idea where to go, then I would be fine on the rest of the trip. I had evidence now that I could do it. I would meet and succeed in whatever new situations came up. I went to bed at peace, eagerly looking forward to my next adventures, knowing that I was being looked after.

DAY 2 ASHTON KEYNES - CRICKLADE

I was happy to have only a short five-mile walk today. I needed a chance to recuperate from my demanding first day on the Path. I slept well last night--in bed at 10:45 p.m. and up at 7:00 a.m.

I enjoyed a leisurely breakfast with four other guests at the B&B. In Bath, I had discovered that the huge English breakfast is not a joke. Some English people really do eat beans and eggs, bacon and sausage, fried potatoes, toast or biscuits, juice, fruit, and possibly cereal, at one meal. In the big kitchen that could comfortably seat ten people, the hostess cooked more eggs, bacon and sausages while we ate. I wasn't tempted by the meat, and I wasn't used to beans for breakfast, but I loved the hearty bread with the excellent English marmalade, both homemade. I was thankful that I wouldn't begin my walk for another three hours.

This was my vision of an ideal B&B--guests from far and near breakfasting together, exchanging information and tales of adventure, the hostess joining in. One couple from Reading, a town about seventy-five miles from Ashton Keynes, was walking their last segment of the Path, having walked the rest of the Path on previous weekends. Since they were traveling upstream, unlike me, I was able to gather valuable information on what I would be encountering. This couple was very keen on the walk, and what was entirely new to me was just another very good hike for them.

At eleven, I set out to find the Path again.

The village of Ashton Keynes stands on both sides of the young Thames River, and the main street follows the river's course. Along here, fish first begin to appear in the Thames and often a footbridge over the water leads to a single grey stone cottage. Frequently, there are three or four steps going down into the shallow water, which can be crossed when there is no flooding. It is said that, during flooding in earlier times, some people left their front and back doors open to allow the water to flow right through their homes.

Ashton Keynes is a perfect example of English village charm and beauty. Though it was late in the year, the English garden flowers--stocks, gladiolas, and asters--were still bestowing their colorful grace upon everyone who took the time to gaze upon them.

As I walked between the houses and along the riverside that wound between them, the place had an air of peace and contentment, like a person "comfortable in his own skin" and grateful for the blessings bestowed upon him. The people seemed particularly kind, gentle, and aware. I had been told that many have moved to the Cotswolds from London, and now commute by train to work there. Or they stay in London during the week and spend their weekends in the villages. It was easy for me to understand why someone would put up with that kind of inconvenience in order to live in such a place. With regret, I said goodbye to Ashton Keynes.

The day was cloudy and windy. Although there were some sunny periods, I wore my windbreaker all day. I was relieved to discover that it was much easier to find my way today. The trail was better marked and truer to the guidebook.

There were many families out, because it was Sunday, I assumed. Some were picnicking, some walking or cycling around the lakes near the Path.

The Cotswold Water Park is a system of over 147 lakes covering forty square miles. The lakes were formed over the last fifty-some years, when the extraction of glacial limestone gravel ceased and the pits naturally filled with water. Now the area is popular for recreation, and is an important winter breeding ground for birds and a home to other wildlife.

I crossed many meadows by the lakes and the still-shallow Thames. Along the path, I fed on the juicy wild blackberries, a favorite fruit of mine. (It was a delightful bonus to find some every day in the rural areas.) As I approached, two rabbits dashed for cover, and a startled deer sprang from its hideout in the shrubbery.

My right shoulder bothered me today. I experimented with adjusting five sets of straps on my backpack to remove some of the weight from my shoulders. I gave up carrying the one-pound guidebook in my hands. Instead, I carried only the torn-out pages I would need for the day, and stashed the rest of the book in my backpack. It never occurred to me that carrying a book all day with my arm in an upright position would place such stress on my arm and shoulder. Added to that, I had been carrying in my hand a bag of leftover food from a cafe along the way. I ate the food, and to lighten my load further, I found a way to fasten my jacket to my backpack when it became too warm to wear. I was always careful to keep the weight as light as possible. As I used up the food I brought with me on the trip, my load became lighter each day--as long as I didn't buy too much food to replace it.

I arrived at Cricklade at two, grateful that I had a place to stay that night. All I had to do was find it. It turned out to be relatively easy. Past the horse competition that was being held just outside of town, I turned right, proceeded to the main street, and there it was. After checking into the White Hart Inn, I asked about the use of a computer and a phone. I was concerned that someone at home might be worrying about me. I was unsuccessful in reaching anyone by phone, and no computer was available. Most businesses were closed on Sundays, except for the pubs and two cafes.

I picked up some fruit, ate a light dinner in my room, carried out my evening practices of laundry, showering, journaling, and meditation, and went to bed early.

DAY 3 CRICKLADE - LECHLADE

Cricklade (population 4,132 in 2001) is a pleasant town with a history as far back as the Iron Age. The grand bell tower of St. Sampson's Church, dating back to the eleventh century, is a dominant landmark today. In Saxon times, Alfred the Great built a system of forts in this area. Now the town is best known for the North Meadow National Nature Reserve, home to the rare snake's head fritillary, a wildflower that appears after flooding.

When I came down from my room that morning, I was still fifteen minutes too early for breakfast, so I set out to explore the town and have a closer look at the architecture. The hotel was one of many eighteenth-century buildings in Cricklade. There is so much charm and character in these old buildings, unlike most of our present-day housing. Or do they just acquire these qualities as they age? I wonder how the buildings of today will appear to our descendants in a few centuries. Will they think our houses have character, or will they seem dull and unimaginative?

When I returned to the Inn I had difficulty determining where I should go for breakfast. I seated myself in the dining room, but there was no one around. In the adjoining bar/lounge, it seemed that the server had not been informed that I was coming. I must have been the only B&B guest there--not what

I expected. The server appeared vague about breakfast, but asked what I would like. There was no fresh fruit on hand, so he went to the market across the street to get some. What first appeared to be a doubtful breakfast turned out to be quite good – cereal, ham and cheese, yogurt, juice, toast, warm croissants, and a terrific fresh fruit bowl. (Coffee was always offered at the B&Bs, but I don't drink it.)

When I left the inn at 8:50 a.m., it was mostly cloudy and threatening rain. Although the day became blustery later, with thunder in the clouds high above, there was no rain. Only about one half of the Path between Cricklade and Lechlade, where I was headed, lies alongside the river.

There were more meadows and bridges to cross before I came to Castle Eaton, a small village where I was expecting to see a castle. There was none, but there was the lovely St. Mary's Church, dating back to the thirteenth century and restored in 1861-63.

I lost my way when I missed a turn and had to backtrack, adding an extra mile. Once again, I called on Spirit for help-- inspiration came--and I realized the mistake I had made. Had I looked on the other side of the gatepost (visible to those coming from the opposite direction), I would have seen the Thames Path marker.

Once, in climbing over a high stile with my backpack, I lost my balance when my pack shifted, and fell backwards into the brambles and stinging nettles. After recovering from my shock, I started to laugh. I must have looked like an upturned turtle. I lay there, considering the best way to move with the least harm from thorns and stings. I decided to undo the straps on my backpack, so I could slip out of it and make it easier to get up. This worked, and the injury was minimal.

As if to balance my stile mishap with some good fortune, I was soon to visit the Saxon church of St. John the Baptist, a short distance off the trail at Inglesham. Dating from around 1205, much of the original building had not been altered. This humble-looking church, with no tower and masonry walls twenty-six inches thick, was quite a contrast to the magnificent splendor of so many English churches. But what it lacked in grandeur, it made up for in atmosphere and authenticity. What may be the original wooden box pews and rough wooden floors, the Jacobean pulpit, and the layers of wall paintings on top of each other, spanning over six hundred years, seemed to carry vibrations from the distant past and convey a sense of privilege to anyone fortunate enough to visit there.

I was awed as I sat down on a wooden bench against the wall to take it all in. Then I noticed a locked wooden donation box on a wall nearby and dropped in some coins in deep appreciation for those who had left this unique church unspoiled.

St. John the Baptist Church is situated just above the meadows near the confluence of the River Coin and the Thames at the Roundhouse (once a lock keeper's house). At this point of the long-disused Thames-Severn Canal, the Thames is deep enough for powered boats to navigate. At this idyllic spot, where huge weeping willows dip their branches down into the water, the remains of an old bridge mark the beginning of the original towpath.

Further on, I could see the arches of the solid-looking Halfpenny Bridge, built in 1782 from Cotswold stone and named after the toll once charged to cross it.

From here, the Path followed the river, and I arrived at St. John's Lock, originally built in 1790, one of forty-five locks built on the Thames. The grounds at the lock were beautifully kept, with manicured grassy areas and brightly colored flowers. On the bank beside the lock was a statue of the reclining figure of bearded Old Father Thames. The statue was commissioned in 1854 for the Crystal Palace exhibition grounds and later moved to the head of the Thames at Kemble, and finally relocated to St. John's Lock. It seemed to be at home, presiding over the river there.

I encountered only one person on the Path that day--a lady walking her dog in a field adjacent to me. At the time I saw her, I had walked and walked without seeing any Thames signs and wasn't sure I was still on the Path. She didn't know about the Path, but helped me to confirm that I was going in the right direction.

The pain in my right shoulder and arm stayed with me all day, and by the time I entered Lechlade, it was bothering me quite a bit. I wasn't sure how I was stressing them. The adjustments I had made to my backpack relieved the pain somewhat, but it didn't really ease until I removed my pack at the end of the day.

The river had been getting progressively deeper as I travelled. Near Lechlade, there were hundreds of swans in the water and on the grass, and now, for the first time, I could see many boats on the water. One of them, the narrowboat, appeared most unusual to me. It was at most seventy-two feet long and seven feet wide--narrow enough to move through the canals. Originally, before there were locks, the men or horses would walk along the riverbank towing these wooden boats. They were used for transporting cargo, and sometimes passengers and mail. In the 1800s, boatmen and their families began to live on the boats. Today, the very modern, steel-hulled narrowboats near Lechlade are used by vacationers and permanent residents.

Lechlade, population around 3100, is an attractive riverside town. The Thames has played a significant role in its history since at least Roman and Saxon times. It was at Lechlade that true commerce began on the Thames. Salt, wool and cheese were shipped from there down the river to Oxford and London. It served as an important trade route for iron goods, copper nails, timber, coal and gunpowder.

My B&B lodging at Lechlade was very different from what I'd had so far. My room was in a building separate from the owner's home, where breakfast was served. After checking in, I left and went for dinner at a pub I had seen along the way. I had discovered that the English pubs (public houses) served simple, reasonably priced meals. Since I usually ate a simple dinner--a salad or stuffed potato--the food was substantial and satisfying.

That evening, I was thrilled to discover that the owners provided a laundry service--no washing by hand for me that night! And another bonus--I was able to use their computer to contact my family.

DAY 4 LECHLADE – NEWBRIDGE - STANDLAKE

The walk to Newbridge was 16 miles. Though the day was mostly sunny, it was cool enough to keep my windbreaker on. As I followed the river and the Thames Path signs, finding my way was easy, except for once, when the signs could be interpreted two ways. A quick check of the guidebook saved me from possible error.

There were remote stretches with no buildings or people in sight--just vast fields, meadows and cow pastures. I wasn't lonely, but I surely was alone.

My sister, a fellow hiker, asked me, one day after I had returned from the trip, what I thought about as I walked. I think she was referring to those times when the terrain changes little for miles and miles and one lapses into reverie. When I wasn't thinking about the sights along the way and my experiences on the Path so far, I often mused over the various places I had walked in the past. I thought about family and friends, and my plan to move to Hawaii the next year.

I must have opened and closed a dozen gates that day--some easy to open, others that I struggled with, and one that I had difficulty even figuring out how it worked.

Periodically, I came to locks, so picturesque with their meticulously kept grounds and neat lock keepers' buildings. I loved to watch the boats sailing up the river and passing through the locks, then anchoring anywhere along the banks. The boaters would simply pound a stake into the ground at the top of the bank and tie the boat up to it.

I always felt blessed to see wildlife; today, I was treated to the sight of some pheasants in the meadow and a blue heron standing beside the river.

In a remote spot, where the Windrush River meets the Thames, the massive, medieval-looking Newbridge Bridge crosses the Thames. Built around 1250, it is thought to be one of England's two oldest bridges. Six pointed arches span the river and an extension of six more were built over the meadow in case of flooding. Even though the bridge is considered inadequate for the volume of present traffic, it is kept as a historical monument.

Near the bridge, the Path left the riverbank and entered the grounds of the Maybush Inn. Across the way stood the sixteenth-century, vine-covered The Rose Revived Inn. I had been told that I would find accommodation for the night at one of these inns. Because I reasoned that both wouldn't be full in September, I hadn't called ahead.

When I crossed the Maybush parking lot and approached the front door, I immediately became concerned. The place felt deserted. Upon entering the lobby, I could see signs of major construction. Two workmen explained that both the Maybush and the Rose Revived were closed due to major damage suffered during recent flooding. June of that year had been one of the wettest months on record in Britain. The Rose

Revived had had one and a half feet of water standing in the pub from the torrential rain.

This was not welcome news. The nearest town where I might stay was Standlake, two miles off the Path. I had already walked over sixteen miles that day, it was now late afternoon, and I still had nowhere to spend the night.

The workmen granted me use of their phone; my guidebook and a brochure at the inn provided some numbers to call. To my great relief and delight, I found a room in a 300- year-old thatched roof cottage in Standlake. At £42, it was pricey for me, but I didn't care. It was the fulfillment of a wish I'd had for this trip to stay in a thatched cottage.

The next challenge now presented itself. To get to Standlake, I would have to walk on the edge of the highway, very hazardous because no shoulder would separate me from the traffic that whizzed by. At the edge of the road was either bushes or a ditch.

I couldn't see any alternative, so I set off. At times, there were only inches between a car and me. With great concentration, I carefully put one foot down in front of the other in order to take up as little room as possible. With my total attention focused in this way, there was no room for fear. (Later, I heard that the Windrush Path could have taken me there, if it was not underwater from flooding.)

With gratitude and great relief, I entered Standlake, an attractive village situated on the Windrush River seven miles west of Oxford. Here too, evidence has been found of Stone and Bronze Age settlements and a pagan burial ground nearby.

I thought it would be easy to find the B&B, but in a style not unusual for me, I went around in circles. I picked up a sandwich at a pub and took it with me for dinner. The spire and bell tower of the English Gothic style St. Giles Church became a landmark that aided me in finally reaching my destination at 6:30 p.m. I estimated I had walked nineteen miles that day (my longest walk), and my shoulders and the soles of my feet echoed my tiredness.

Pinkhill Cottage was a four-star B&B oozing with character. The owner thought that, at one time, three buildings had been joined together, and the part where I stayed (with a date of 1788 on the outside wall) consisted of a sitting room, a bedroom and bath that had originally been the stable and hayloft. I loved my bedroom, with its low oak- beamed ceilings and walls, and the floor that sloped noticeably all the way to the outer wall of the bathroom. The low barn-styled bathroom door opened uphill, so that I had to tug to open it and duck as I entered.

I fell asleep wondering what life was like for those who first lived in this dwelling. What might they have thought if they could see that their stable and hayloft had become an expensive guesthouse three hundred years later?

DAY 5 STANDLAKE – NEWBRIDGE - OXFORD

I had a notion in my head, before this trip, that B&Bs were fairly standard. In the places where I had stayed in North America, there was usually a central dining room where breakfast was served. The hostess was often nearby, in and out of the kitchen to serve, and inquire how things were and, occasionally, to sit down to chat.

Here in England, so far, every B&B had been different. In Standlake, I had my own sitting room, which served as my breakfast room. There I sat on the morning of my fifth day, reading while I waited impatiently for my breakfast to be served at eight-thirty. The hostess brought in my breakfast, and I ate without seeing or hearing anyone else. I felt quite isolated and disappointed. One of the benefits and pleasures of a B&B, for me, is the social aspect--meeting the hosts and guests, exchanging travel stories, and getting acquainted with people from other lands and cultures.

I was anxious to get going; I had two miles to go just to get back on the Path, and then fourteen miles to Oxford. I quickly ate my breakfast, then felt bold enough to ask if I could get a ride with anyone who was going to Newbridge that morning. The hostess knew of a possibility – she tried to contact a friend while I waited, watching the time. I didn't want to wait too long – better to be walking than sitting there, and then not having a ride after all.

A half-hour passed. Finally, at nine-thirty, arrangements were made for a ride. I gave a prayer of thanks, grateful that I would save some time and not have to walk the highway again. After a five-minute ride back to Newbridge, I was ready to pick up the trail where I had left off.

The weather was cloudy, windy, and threatening rain all day, but a good temperature for walking. It was easy to follow the trail—there were only a couple of times that I had to pause to double-check the guidebook.

I felt fully recuperated from my long day yesterday, except for my still-sore shoulder and arm. Thinking that I may have overstressed my right shoulder by always lifting my backpack from that side, I began to alternate sides.

Many boats, most of them moored, were on the river today. The narrowboats appeared to be lived in. They were about six feet wide, tapering to narrower roofs with pots of flowers growing on them. A lady on shore offered to give me a boat ride to the next lock down the river. Regretfully, I declined. I would love to have chatted with her, but I reminded myself that I had set out to walk the Path, not ride.

I traversed countless gates between fields and pastures along the River. I had to tread carefully to avoid stepping in the cow pies, as we called them in Saskatchewan. With all my slowing down to sightsee, as well as the gates to open and close, and the cow pies to watch out for, I was averaging only two and a half miles an hour.

The Path followed the river most of the day, with only one stretch near Bablock Hythe where it departed when the towpath switched river sides. It was not unusual for the Path to cross to the other side of the river if, as in this case, there were water meadows to avoid.

At Eyesham Lock, another well-kept lock with plenty of picnic and bench seats, a public footpath led over a weir. I debated taking it, but decided not to spend the time. Each lock seemed to have something special. Kings Lock, with its immaculate gardens, had grassy areas that could be used for camping.

To the left of the Path, I passed Port Meadows, flood meadows northwest of Oxford which contain ancient free grazing land that has never been ploughed. Alfred the Great gave three hundred acres of pasture to the Freemen of Oxford. The Meadows contain well-preserved evidence of Bronze Age barrows and an Iron Age settlement.

From the center of Oxford, Folly Bridge--a stone bridge over the Thames erected in1825-27--carries Abingdon Road south. The two parts of the bridge are separated by an island. It is not certain how the bridge got its name. It apparently stands at the site of the ford over which oxen crossed at one time. The first known stone bridge here was built around 1085.

By the end of the day, my shoulder was much better. I attributed this improvement to a couple of pack adjustments and to the affirmations I repeated aloud for two miles: "My shoulder and arm are in perfect condition." The pain completely disappeared as I affirmed, but returned later, until I again relieved it with the affirmations.

I arrived at Oxford at four-thirty. After a little searching, using my guidebook for contact numbers, I found a very basic hotel room for £40 night in an old building that was attached to another building. The shared bathroom was up a flight of stairs from my room. I didn't relish the thought of going up and down those deserted stairs to the bathroom during the night, nor did the odor of smoke in my room appeal to me, but I was grateful for the clean bed, and the fact that I was almost straight across the street from the entrance to the Thames Path.

For dinner at a nearby restaurant, I asked the server for raw mushrooms in my salad. He thought he hadn't heard me correctly. Apparently, the English never eat mushrooms uncooked. Nevertheless, the chef obliged, and the terrific made-to-order green salad left me feeling content and looking forward to my tour of Oxford the next morning.

DAY 6 OXFORD - ABINGDON

Oxford is fifty miles northwest of London, and had a population of 150,200 as of 2011. It is situated on a gravel plateau almost entirely encircled by water. The Thames, where it flows through Oxford, is known as the Isis.

Some believe that Oxford was first settled by the Saxons to establish a fort for a river crossing for oxen. Another source says Oxford may have been built in 1009 BC by Memphric, king of the Britons. If this is so, Oxford would be one of the most ancient cities in the world.

Oxford almost entirely escaped bombing during the Second World War. It was said that Hitler spared Oxford because he thought he might one day have headquarters there, but according to a report found in the Oxford University Library in 2013, Hitler's plans to bomb Oxford were cancelled when they were no longer viable.

Oxford is well known for its rowing team and its prowess in other sports. It was here at Iffley Track that Roger Bannister, formerly an Oxford medical student, set the four-minute mile record in 1954. But Oxford has been changing. Now one of the fastest growing cities in Britain, it has a diverse economic base, from publishing to manufacturing and technology.

When I planned my Thames River Path trip, I allotted fifteen days for walking and left three days unassigned, in case I needed to extend the walk, or take rest days. I had already used one of those extra days when it took me two days instead of one to travel from the Source to Cricklade. In my plan, I had also allotted a few hours to do some sightseeing in Oxford.

This morning, as I sat near the front of the upper level of the Oxford tour bus, the windows were open and I was freezing. Other passengers didn't seem to mind the cold wind. Adding to my discomfort was the inadequate sound system, which made it very hard for me to understand what the tour-guide/driver was saying. I was able to shrug that off, thinking that I wouldn't remember all that he said anyhow. Still, there were times when I would like to have known what building I was looking at. Thankfully, the harmonious architecture of the impressive buildings took my mind off both the cold and the communication problems.

I had seen many photos of Oxford. I could understand why it was called "The City of the Dreaming Spires." Someone described them as gentle spires. Before my trip, I hadn't known that Oxford College was made up of thirty-eight individual colleges and six separate educational institutions. I thought there was one huge campus---not separate colleges spread over the city. I learned that writers Lewis Carroll, Kenneth Grahame, C. S. Lewis, T. E. Lawrence, and Oscar Wilde were students at Oxford.

Most of the men walking on the city streets were in suits and ties. Oxford seemed ultra conservative and serious, for dedicated people with purpose. However, that was only my impression from a tour bus. I actually saw little of the city. Others have described Oxford as vibrant and cosmopolitan.

Before I left Oxford, I needed to find accommodations for the night in Abingdon, ten miles away. Because I had little success using the public phone, I found my way to the Tourist Information Center, where they phoned a B&B hotline and tracked down a room for me at £35. I considered myself blessed to find a modest room with shared bathroom at that price; the available hotel rooms were as much as £73. Apparently, some people who had been flooded out of their homes that summer had moved into the B&Bs, and other local rooms had been filled by those attending a big music festival in Abingdon.

I didn't get started until after twelve-thirty. The weather was very changeable all day---showers, wind, a few sunny periods, then warm. To find the Path again, I headed in the direction of the river and followed it until I saw some Thames Path signs. It turned out to be a very easy day for finding my way. I stopped once to rearrange my backpack load to ease the stress I was feeling on my back. Later I became aware of a soreness in the ankle area of my right foot. Loosening my bootlaces and rearranging the boot tongue and my sock didn't solve the problem. The pain, from my ankle down through the inside of my foot, increased during the afternoon, and by nightfall, it was very sore and uncomfortable to walk on.

Although there were many out walking that day, I encountered only one, possibly two, people who appeared to be doing the Thames River Path.

I reached Iffley Meadows, ancient water meadows that flood every year, and the nearby Iffley Lock, built as it is today in 1924. There were many weirs along this stretch of the river, among them the Stanford Weirs, which were difficult to see from the Path.

The Path led away from the river as I neared Abingdon and returned again at Abingdon Bridge. The original bridge, built in 1422, has largely been rebuilt during the last century. The long, medieval-looking bridge across the wide expanse of river presented a picture-perfect entrance to Abingdon.

Abingdon was a flourishing agricultural center in the thirteenth and fourteenth centuries, and is still a market town. It is one of the most important of the historic towns on the Thames; it is said that people have lived there for over 6000 years.

There is a strange, long-standing tradition in the town of throwing buns from the County Hall roof on specific days of celebration while crowds assemble in the market square below. More recent bun-throwing ceremonies took place to celebrate the wedding of Prince William and Catherine Middleton in 2011, and the Diamond Jubilee of Elizabeth II in 2012.

I arrived at my B&B around five-thirty. My room was on the top floor of an old and charming building. As I looked down on the owner picking fall apples from a backyard tree, I once again felt a connection to my Canadian roots. I lived for twenty-seven years in the Okanagan Valley, well known for its apples.

That night, my ankle was so sore, I wondered if I would be able to continue on the Path the next day. I lay in bed, puzzled as to why one foot was sore and not the other, and why it was sore on the inside. How was I stressing it? I tried to think of all the possibilities. That boot was the same as the other boot; why that foot only? I reviewed the day, and when my foot bothered me the most. And then I knew--it was the way I had been navigating the deep, narrow cow trails on the Path. They were not wide enough to place both feet at the bottom of the trail as I walked, so I would place my right foot at an awkward angle on the side of the rut, while my left foot was level in the bottom. The unnatural position placed a strain on my foot, and the boot rubbing against my ankle caused the soreness. Some ice and healing exercises brought relief.

DAY 7 ABINGDON - WALLINGFORD

Here was the B&B of my imaginings--one large table in a cosy dining room and a breakfast of fresh fruit salad, yogurt, a variety of cereals (including the host's homemade granola), and freshly baked bread. Orders were also being taken from the kitchen. At the husband's urging (I think he was proud of his wife's cooking), I ordered mushrooms and tomatoes, and stressed to my host that I would like them only slightly cooked. They arrived as ordered, deliciously seasoned.

I enjoyed chatting with a couple at the table who were from Edmonton, Canada, in the province next to mine. The wife, a research engineer with a world-wide oil company, was taking training in England, and her husband was on vacation.

When I started my walk at nine, it was cloudy and quite windy, but warm. From the Path on the opposite side of the river, I turned for one last lingering view of lovely Abingdon.

My foot had recovered well overnight, and another pack adjustment in the afternoon greatly eased my back. I was getting stronger; my spirits were good, and I was managing to stay on an even keel, that is, not getting too excited when things went right, nor too upset when things went wrong. I quickened my pace today. Head down, watching my footing, and chanting, "Om, Peace," I went for it.

As I neared Culham, a town with more than twelve centuries of history, across the fields I could see the Culham Manor House with its church, cottages and pub assembled around a green field--another delightful English countryside snapshot. I was amused to note the names of three Culham pubs: "Nag's Head," "Sow and Pigs," and "Waggon and Horses." The town is known, however, not for its pubs, but for the Culham Lab, a leading fusion research lab nearby.

After days of miles and miles of meadows and fields, the villages along the way were a nice change.

Past Clifton Lock, a rough narrow way by the edge of the fields opened out and suddenly, across a meadow, the red-brick Gothic bridge and the church spire of St. Michaels Church at Clifton Hampden, another old village, came into view. I left the Path and crossed the meadow to find the village post office. In order to lighten the weight I carried, I wanted to mail the pages from my guidebook that were no longer needed, plus some post cards and brochures I had picked up, to my home in Canada.

(To fast-forward to my arrival back at my home in Victoria-- When I picked up my mail, I noticed that the envelope had been resealed. Examination revealed that thirty-three guidebook pages and a couple of brochures were missing. Strange! One can only guess why someone would steal them, or even open the envelope in the first place.)

I would love to have taken more time to explore Clifton Hampden. This unique village has several cottages that were built in the sixteenth and early seventeenth centuries, many still thatched. At the top of a steep bank stood the church I had seen from the distance. It was another one of those times when I debated--should I or shouldn't I stop to have a closer look? I checked my watch and kept going.

A little later, I was again regretting my shortage of time. I had to decide against a side-trip to Dorchester, a historic market town, where the remains of a Roman wall can still be seen, in order to get to Wallingford by four-thirty, when the Tourist Information Bureau closed.

Except for a couple of puzzling turns in direction today, which I was able to reason out, the Path was pretty straightforward. There were many beautiful little villages crowded into the thirteen and a half miles that I covered, with fewer fields and meadows, but many locks and bridges, and more pillboxes.

The pillboxes, named after their shape, are concrete or brick fortified structures built by the British to protect London from possible German invasion during World War II. Some 1200 pillboxes are still to be found in England, many along the Thames. Most of the eight to ten that I saw are now covered with undergrowth, and some are roosts for bats.

Just before the medieval bridge at Shillingford, I slowly and carefully passed through the first kissing gate I had encountered on the Path, making sure I could do so without removing my backpack. Kissing gates, built to keep out livestock, allow only one person at a time to pass through. The pair of gates touch (kiss) when closed. Apparently, there is no romantic origin to the name.

At the hamlet of Shillingford, on the corner of a cottage very close to the river, was a flood marker which indicated that the highest water level from flooding--well above my head--occurred in 1809. I recalled seeing flood markings at a similar height on a tree along the river on the approach to Clifton Hampden.

Not far from Shillingford Bridge, the distant Chiltern Hills could be seen across the open fields. The Chilterns area is a chalk escarpment, 324 square miles of superb scenery, secluded villages, and thriving market towns. In 1965, it was officially designated as an Area of Outstanding Beauty.

The Benson weir and lock were very impressive. The original lock was built out of oak in 1788, and rebuilt with masonry in 1870. The present lock keeper's house is one century old. A footbridge crosses the millstream, and then moves above the thundering waters of the weir.

Entering Wallingford, I headed straight for the Tourist Information Bureau. Alas, even though it was only 3:55, the place was already closed. I walked around, asking people for leads to B&Bs, but couldn't find those to which I was directed. Inquiry at a couple of hotels revealed that one was £75 a night, the other fully booked. After checking my guidebook, I phoned a listed B&B--success! Why hadn't I looked there first? The one that I had phoned earlier from Abingdon was unavailable, so I had made an assumption that other places would be full. Poor reasoning.

I had completed my first week on the Path – a lot of learning, trial and error, adjustments, lessons in humility, wondrous sights, and new experiences – all in all, a terrific week.

DAY 8 WALLINGFORD - TILEHURST

This morning, I shared the breakfast table with a lady from Sussex, probably in her fifties, taking three days to do sections of the Path upstream from me. I hadn't yet met anyone walking the Path "all at once," like myself. I assumed that those I have seen along the way without a sizable backpack were not likely walking the entire 184-mile Path.

Two miles from Wallingford, the Path led past Chelsey, another village with Bronze Age origins. In a church graveyard there lies the grave of novelist Agatha Christie, who died in 1976.

Today, the weather was perfect, warm enough to roll my pants up into capris and go without a jacket. Many people were about--strolling, sailing, fishing on the river--taking advantage of the unseasonably warm day. For the first time, I saw canoeists on the Thames, and today and yesterday, I watched rowers training on the river. They were directed by a man with a blowhorn, who followed in a boat or sailed alongside them.

For some idyllic moments, I sat on a bench by the river, eating my lunch. A light breeze played over me as I watched people come and go on the sidewalk that separated me from the river, and listened to two men on their narrowboat decks discussing their boat-top gardens.

This lunch spot was a pleasant change. Up until now, if I was hungry around noon, I would begin to watch for a dry, sheltered spot just off the Path where I could sit down and stretch out to relax, away from rain, wind, cattle, sheep and any other possible disturbances. I usually lunched on a half-sheet of nori with nut butter, dried or fresh fruit, and energy bars, supplemented with Cell Food, chlorella, and maca. In the mornings, I would stop for a snack break after walking for one and a half to two hours. In the afternoons, if I had eaten a late lunch, or arrived at my destination by three, I would omit the break.

The Path now followed its usual errant ways, crossing bridges, moving away from the river, into wooded areas, and through a narrow tunnel of hedges as it proceeded to Goring on the north bank and Streatley on the south. The two villages are connected by Goring and Streatley Bridge. The current bridge, completed in 1923, replaced the old timber bridge built in 1837. Here the Goring Gap constricts the Thames as it flows through the narrowest part of the Thames River Valley.

The Ridgeway, another national long distance trail, passes through Streatley near the juncture of two of the oldest tracks in Britain, the Icknield Way and the Ridgeway, which meet on the Goring side of the river. In the earliest days, and before ferries, travelers would have been able to cross here if the water wasn't too high.

Goring has many old religious sites. Early in the twelfth century, the Church of England parish church of St. Thomas of Canterbury was built. In the fifteenth century, the bell tower was added, with one of its eight bells dating from 1290. The wood of the carved rood screen that separates the chancel from the nave was taken from a ship in Nelson's fleet at Trafalgar.

Shortly after Goring, the Path made a wide detour onto a track that led up a steep, roughly wooded bank with a great view of the Thames beyond. More climbing took me up some terraced steps on a long steep graveled hill. The steps were so far apart and the path so steep, I soon had to sit down to rest. When trying to get up again, I couldn't get a footing; my backpack weighed me down and my boots kept slipping on the scree between the widely spaced steps. I tried removing my backpack, but couldn't place it where it would be within reach when I stood up. At last, I sat down on a step and did what I usually did when in trouble--called on Spirit for help. Then, with determination and a mighty effort, I tried once again to stand without slipping back. Though somewhat unsteady, this time I was on my way--over the top of the hill and down onto the road to Whitchurch.

From a village street, the Path turned right onto a church drive and passed a lychgate, a covered gateway found at the entrance to some traditional English churchyards. (In the Middle Ages, when people were buried only in shrouds, not coffins, the priest would conduct the first part of the funeral at the lychgate.)

At the Whitchurch Bridge, I stopped to read the historic tariff poster at the side of the road. Once on the bridge, I looked back for another picture-book view of the Thames area--the river, the honey-colored cottages visible through the trees, the church, and the mill.

The Path passed through Pangbourne Meadow and came to Mapledurham Lock, a lovely spot where I stopped to wander through the art gallery. At the adjoining tea hut, I treated myself to ice cream. I loved the simple, quaint, unexpected delights that I encountered when traveling in England.

Soon, I approached Tilehurst and left the Path to walk through the town to my B&B. On the phone that morning, I had asked the owner if she lived close to the river; she replied in the affirmative. Wrong question! "Close" is a relative term. It was two miles--not a short distance for me at the end of a fifteen-mile day.

At the house, I was met at the door by a man who explained that his wife had to be away for the night (apparently she had forgotten this when she took the reservation), and he would understand if I no longer wanted to stay there. Quickly, I thought about it. I was tired and didn't want to go looking for another place. I intuitively felt he was safe. Deciding to take the risk, I agreed to stay. That being settled, I dropped off my backpack in my room, and left to find a place to eat dinner.

I headed for the closest place that sold food--an Indian Tandori restaurant just down the road that I had passed earlier. I would have loved a green salad; I didn't want cooked food then. (I tried to eat as much of my food raw as possible--my usual diet at home. That day, I had had one slice of melon, toast and fresh tomatoes for breakfast, the usual raw nuts, dried fruit, nori, and goji berries throughout the day and, of course, the delicious ice cream bar treat that afternoon.)

Though I was tired, I wasn't complaining. I would shortly be in bed.

DAY 9 TILEHURST - HENLEY

I made it safely through the night without anxiety over my solo status with the male stranger in the house. Downstairs in the morning, he welcomed me to the lovely continental breakfast he had prepared. He appeared right at home in the kitchen, and with the present situation. It probably wasn't the first time he had experienced it. He invited me to help myself to fresh grapes, bananas, apples, and wholegrain toast with… peanut butter! I had been "asking" for peanut better--I love it, and I hadn't had any since I left home.

At 9:20, I started on the two-mile walk back to the Path. From there, it would be another twelve miles to Henley-on-Thames, where I would spend the night. Leaving Tilehurst behind, the Path led away from the railway lines it had been following and moved into open fields and a measure of seclusion--but not for long.

Caversham Bridge came into sight. This bridge crossed over from Reading, a large town at the confluence of the Thames and the River Kennet, to the suburb of Caversham. The Path led through a tunnel under the bridge. Later, Horseshoe Bridge took me across the spot where the Kennet flows into the Thames.

The Path continued on by the Thames, then wound by a wetlands nature reserve and through some trees to Sonning

Lock. Brightly colored flowers filled window boxes and seemed to wave gaily from everywhere on the attractive grounds. Across the narrow Sonning Bridge on the north side of the river, another bridge crossed a weir stream, where there had once stood an eighteenth century flour mill, now the site of a theatre and restaurant.

Once out of the populated areas, the Path looped through verdant countryside, providing continuous visual delight. Shiplake, a small village with a cluster of cottages and a church, could be seen on higher ground, but the towpath continued along a meadow, through a kissing gate, and into a paved track leading to Shiplake Lock.

Up from the lock, I crossed to the opposite bank at Lashbrook (no longer a ferry crossing), and cut inland through Lower Shiplake. The path took me between gardens to a tree-lined road and upscale houses. At one house, a miniature railway and railway station circled the garden.

A fenced path continued to Marsh Lock. Along a nearby meadow, iron studs were placed in 1903 to define the fourteen-foot width of the towpath. Only one remains, an indication of the bank's erosion.

Today seemed to be a series of bridges and gates, twists and turns, going quickly from meadows to populated areas.

There was mixed cloud and sun, and a cool wind that helped to keep it from becoming too warm at times. I had a very good day walking, my fastest and best yet. I discovered that I had been placing the waist straps of my backpack too low, accounting for some of the strain on my shoulders the past few days. Now, with the belts tightly cinched directly over my hipbones, a lot of weight was removed from my shoulders.

The approach to Henley-on-Thames was very lovely and serene, the stuff of painters. I liked to see so many people out and about (as they are on a pleasant Sunday in my own country)--fishing, rowing, sailing, and strolling with or without their dogs. They do love their dogs here!

I had been eagerly waiting to see Henley. Although I had little previous knowledge of most of the towns and villages on the Path so far, I knew of Henley. The mental pictures I had probably came from photos and movies I had seen--men in striped jackets and boater hats, rowers competing in the regattas, crowds everywhere.

Henley-on-Thames was the site of the first boat races between Oxford and Cambridge, and each summer, the Royal Regatta is held there. The rowing course starts at Temple Island in the middle of the river not far from Henley. The towpath, for part of the way near here, has a paved surface, provided for the coaches of rowing crews to cycle along.

In the nineteenth century, Henley was so popular as a summer destination that it was compared to Piccadilly Circus in London at rush hour. Many actors, writers, and singers have lived at Henley and been buried there--among them George Orwell, Prince Stanislaw Albrecht Radziwill, and Dusty Springfield. In 1970, Beatle George Harrison purchased and restored Friar Park, a 120-room Victorian Neo-Gothic mansion, and lived there until his death.

I wasn't very tired when I arrived in Henley at two, even though (against my earlier resolve to avoid carbs), I gave in to temptation and ate a piece of "fruit" cake from a tearoom at one of the locks. Contrary to the guidebook information, the Tourist Info Center in Henley was already closed. Fortunately, my B&B host that morning had given me names and phone numbers for two B&Bs that I might try in Henley. Rather than look for a phone, I found my way to the addresses and knocked on the doors. Both were fully occupied, but the second owner kindly offered to phone around for me. All he could find was a pricey double room, at £55. I thought I'd better take it. Later, I learned that this room was available only because the existing reservation had been cancelled that morning. Consequently, that night I enjoyed a lovely ensuite room with all the amenities.

After treating myself again after dinner, with cheesecake for dessert, I cautioned myself to watch the slippery slope of carbs that zap my energy and are detrimental to my health, and made a mental note to pick up some healthy sugar-free energy bars the next day.

I chatted with the bartender who took my dinner order. He was interested in my Canadian background and couldn't help comparing Canadians to Americans.

DAY 10 HENLEY - MARLOW

This morning, as usual, I was rested and recovered from the day before, and eager to set foot on the Path. A good breakfast always helps to start my day off well. I lucked out again with peanut butter, which I added to banana to make my favorite sandwich. Some raisins, Vega smoothie mix in my juice, and I was satisfyingly full for a few hours.

Around four to six this morning, the weather had been stormy, but by the time my host dropped me off at eight-thirty, not far from the Thames trail, the wind had calmed down. It was raining lightly, but it ceased later and it became warm enough for me to remove my rain pants and jacket.

The Thames Path crosses Henley Bridge on a reach between Hambledon Lock and Marsh Lock. This stone road bridge with five elliptical arches was built in 1786 to replace an earlier wooden structure. Sculptures of the faces of Isis and Tamesis (an ancient name for the Thames) are on the keystones of the central arch on each side of the bridge, Isis facing upstream and Tamesis downstream.

Early in the day, I took a wrong turn, adding an extra mile and a half or so to the nine-mile trip to Marlow, my destination. Although I get impatient with myself, and frustrated, when I can't figure out where I went wrong, I'm really not too concerned when I make these errors, so long as it's not too late in the day and I have a reservation for the night.

Down the long Henley regatta stretch, beyond Temple Island with its tiny temple, the river bends sharply towards Hambledon Lock, built in 1773. The picturesque Hambledon Mill, with views across the weirs, is now divided into flats. There is a story about an eccentric lock keeper who lived in a small brick house at the lock for fifty-nine years. It is said that he made bread for the bargemen, ate onion porridge at night, and walked every day to Hambledon to mark a cross on the ground.

The Path left the riverside for short distances to pass through open fields with breath-taking views of the Thames Valley. It has been said that nowhere is the Thames more magnificent than between Henley and Marlow. One lovely view was that of Culham Court, a red-brick eighteenth-century Queen Anne house on the rise across the river one and a half miles from the Thames. This house was sometimes visited by royalty in the nineteenth century.

More open meadows, fenced on one side, led to a track, some cottages, over a field, and back to the Thames. Along the way, there were several gates, footbridges to cross, traces of a ferry landing. Then I came to the prosperous village of Medenham. Across the river, the remains of twelfth-century Medenham Abbey lie near the present eighteenth-century Abbey, now a private residence.

Another shortcut and I was back on the towpath. Then more open meadows on the outskirts of Hurley, one of them popular for picnics and the other for recreation, such as cricket. The weir at Hurley Lock attracts freestyle kayakers.

The Path led over a stream, past cottages, and into Hurley village. There, two tithe barns had been converted into houses, one with a circular fourteenth-century dovecote next to it. Further up the street was the Old Bell, a hotel and pub founded in 1135 as a hostelry of Hurley Priory.

Another bridge, another lock, and soon Bisham Abbey appeared across the river. The present Tudor house, now a National Sports Center, was built using fragments of the original abbey. Bisham Church, with its seventeenth-century tower, is right by the waterside. Another bend, and the fine line of the suspension bridge at Marlow and a nearby pinnacled church spire provided another lovely English scene.

Marlow has been an important historic town due to its location on the Thames. Even by 1227, it had its own market. Marlow has attracted many sports enthusiasts. It is home to the top rowing club in Britain, at which Olympic oarsman Sir Steve Redgrave trained. There are also cricket, rugby, football and other sport clubs. Another claim to fame for Marlow is that it was once home to Percy Bysshe Shelley.

Lots of birds around today. I was surprised to see Canada Geese in Marlow and Henley. I didn't realize they were to be found in England. The large population of swans was very tame where they were being fed by people, and the pheasants in the woods were so numerous, they were becoming a nuisance.

A highlight of the day occurred when I was heading down a back lane away from the river. A number of reddish-colored birds, around twelve, were soaring and swooping over adjacent fields. Their movements made me think they were eagles or in the eagle family, but I learned from a passing cyclist that they were red kites. I stopped and watched for a while, wondering why they kept circling that field. Later, while waiting in the Tourist Information Center, I was surprised to find brochures advertising red kite-watching tours. Apparently, these tours were similar to whale watching tours, in that sometimes you were fortunate to spot the animal and sometimes you weren't. I felt honored and blessed to have seen them, and without having to search.

It was a good day. I was stronger and walking faster. My shoulder and arm were feeling much better since I found the right placement and adjustment for my backpack straps. The pack itself felt quite comfortable, and lighter.

When heading up the street to the Tourist Center, I happened upon an organic restaurant and a health food store, side by side. What a bonanza! I purchased energy bars and organic dates, and ate a fresh green salad and a brownie. Such a treat!

I arrived at my room at five-thirty--a twin room with shared bath for £45. Since I had already had dinner, I enjoyed a rare relaxing evening watching TV while I sipped a cup of tea and wrote in my journal.

Here is an excerpt from my journal:

"So many, many beautiful scenes, spots, churches, bridges. It's impossible to cite them all. There are so many every day-- I'm not going to try to describe them-- – I couldn't; sometimes they leave me speechless. I love watching the river life – people on their boats, the canoeists and rowers, the fishers on the banks, the ducks and swans."

DAY 11 MARLOW - WINDSOR

I had a breakfast of grapefruit and a Vega-supplement smoothie and put together a tomato sandwich to eat on the trail--seemed like a good idea to have it later. As I started out at 8:10 and reached the Path at 8:35, I felt good. But an hour after eating three-quarters of the sandwich (pseudo whole grain bread), I was draggy and tired. I knew then that I had to stop eating breads for breakfast--they zapped my energy.

From Marlow Bridge to Marlow Lock, there is no towpath. Before locks were built here, barges were hauled up the river by manpower, or by using a long towline to horses, which were led down a twisty, turning path.

The Path bends this way and that: along a road back to the riverside, past a mill, more bends, a gravel path, and then under a bridge. There were boathouses by the path, villas on the slopes, and a genuine, but rather small, castle with turrets and battlements. From the slopes of Winter Hill nearby, one could have an exquisite view of the scene below--the stately avenue of poplars near playing fields and picnic benches, the open meadows, and the ever-intriguing river.

Coming off a detour, I turned to go along the river. Something didn't feel right, but not trusting my instincts, I kept going until at last I felt sure I wasn't on the Path. Retracing my steps, I discovered that I had made a wrong turn and was walking upstream, in the direction from which I had come. I estimated that I had lost an hour. As usual when such incidents occur, I had mixed feelings of self-chastisement for my error and gratitude that I had found my way again.

On a broad track near the Thames, the Path continued to Bourne End, a favorite reach for dinghy sailing. Minutes later, it passed through a gate into the National Trust-owned Cock Marsh. This marshland between Winter Hill and the Thames has been common land since 1272 and is still used as grazing land.

A bend brings into view the Cookham Bridge and the sixteenth-century Norman tower of Holy Trinity Church, now restored. Cookham is a very popular riverside resort. One interesting note is that the traditional Swan Upping Ceremony takes place here. This is the time when the Royal Swankeeper captures the new cygnets and determines ownership, while establishing a swan census. Another interesting fact about Cookham is that writer Kenneth Graham and artist Stanley Spencer lived here.

Below the bridge, where the Thames flows into at least four channels, the Path moved away from the river into open fields, between hedges, through woodlands and Beachwood stands, past elegant estate colleges and the Cliveden Estate. Along the reach, the colors of autumn provided beautiful variety.

Walking on, I came to Boulter's Lock, a very popular spot for the fashionable in Edwardian Days. By the lock, a bridge leads to Ray Mill Island, four acres of delight for a weary city-dweller. But the Path bypasses it, and soon crosses Maidenhead Bridge, going through gates, another boatyard, by Brunel's masterpiece railway bridge, and later past Bray Lock.

More open fields to Dorney Lake, home to the Eton College Rowing Club and one of the 2012 Olympic sites. Across the river, Oakley Court can be seen--a Victorian Gothic country house built in 1859, currently a luxury hotel. Its Gothic architecture lends itself well to movie-making. It has been the location for many horror films, such as "The Bride of Dracula" in 1962.

Alone by the river, away from nearby Boveney hamlet, sits the simple St. Mary Magdalene Boveney chapel, with walls of chalk rubble. It contains fifteenth and sixteenth-century pews and church bells, and a small, probably twelfth-century, lancet window.

Passing Boveney Lock, there is a track at the river with a low platform, a bench, and a low weathered tablet that states that this is Athens, bathing place for the boys from Eton. It reads: "Boys who are undressed must either get at once into the water or get behind the screens when boats containing ladies come into sight."

Another footbridge, a grassy bank on a river loop, under a road bridge, a railway bridge, a glimpse of Windsor Castle, and then, as I entered Brocas meadow, the castle came into full view. The sight of the huge Ferris wheel to my right and the majestic castle just beyond seemed so incongruous.

I left the Brocas by a gate and came out at the foot of Eton High Street. The Eton College buildings could be seen up to the left, but the Path turned right over a pedestrian bridge into Windsor.

As I proceeded down the streets of Windsor, the rain was coming down in torrents--as if someone above with a huge tank was just dumping it down. The water poured down the drainpipes and ran over the streets on its way to the gutters. Carefully, through my rain-covered glasses, I placed my steps. Even when I removed my glasses, it wasn't much better. I was disappointed that I couldn't see much of the town; it was all I could do to read the map that the Tourist Information Center in Marlow had given me. I don't know how I would have found my B&B without the map. But once again, I was thankful for my dependable waterproof rain gear and a room reservation for the night.

My room in the century-old Victorian house was very small (which didn't matter to me), with a shared, modern bathroom. Eileen, the hostess, was a very talkative, interesting character. The B&B hosts I had encountered so far, had been amiable, but hadn't had much to say unless I initiated conversation.

Windsor was not what I expected; I had thought it would be more like London. Windsor is more sophisticated than the villages on the Thames, but in my view, not at all cosmopolitan.

Windsor Castle, in particular, surprised me. It was the first real castle I had seen; never did I expect to see one with a wall bordering a city street. I had a better view of the castle the next day when it wasn't raining, and thought it very impressive. It covers more than thirteen acres and is the oldest and largest occupied castle in the world, home to British kings and queens for almost a thousand years. The original castle was built in the eleventh century by William the Conquerer after the Norman invasion, to protect the Normans and provide a lookout from a strategic part of the Thames. Much later, when London was being bombed during World War II, the Royal Family spent some time there. Now it appears to be a favorite weekend home for Elizabeth II.

The town of Old Windsor was nationally important in the Middle Ages and became one of the wealthiest towns in England. Its close association with royalty brought many opportunities to boost trade and commerce. Geoffrey Chaucer worked at Windsor Castle in 1391 as "Clerk of the Works."

A modern note: Legoland Park in Windsor is the largest of its kind in the world, and the only one in Great Britain.

DAY 12 WINDSOR - SHEPPERTON

What an interesting, diverse day! I walked the Path. I walked the highway. I bussed.

The day started off cloudy, but without rain. Today, I got a better look at Windsor and the castle. As I walked through the village around eight-thirty, the shopkeepers were setting out their wares. At the bakery, I was astonished to see the window shelves piled high with mouth-watering buns, croissants, cakes and pastries. Yesterday, when I passed it around four p.m., there were so few baked goods on the shelves that I wondered how the place could stay open. Now I understood that, rather than being a failing business, it must be very prosperous. Everything looked so good; I was very tempted to buy, but remembered my decision to stay away from bread for breakfast. To be truthful, I think what really prevented me from succumbing to temptation was that it was too hard for me to choose from all those delectable-looking goodies.

From Windsor Bridge, the Thames took a loop around the open area of Home Park. I looked back across the fields and stood there admiring the view of Windsor Castle from that side. Without the rain, it appeared serene and stately standing there in its expanse of manicured grounds and well-placed shrubbery.

The Path crossed Victoria Bridge, moved away from the riverside, back to the Thames, under Albert Bridge, up a slope to cross a bridge and then turned down steps to get back on the towpath. Can you imagine trying to follow the path without a guidebook--or plentiful signs? But such is the Thames River Path. I am in awe of the ingenuity and the determination of the Ramblers' Association in constructing that continuous trail so close to the river.

As the Path diverted from the main river channel, I came to a locked gate proclaiming that the Thames River Path was closed due to hoof and mouth disease in the area. I vaguely recalled hearing something about the problem here, but didn't get the impression it was still current. I remembered the time, growing up in Saskatchewan, Canada, when the disease was rampant in livestock and our own cattle were at risk. Now in Britain, many footpaths were closed as a precaution, to help prevent the spread of the highly infectious disease and reduce the loss of animals.

I concluded this must be an old sign that no one had bothered to take down. (Amazing how we sometimes choose to think what is expedient for us.) So, not to be deterred, I slithered under the gate and proceeded along a fenced field that joined a drive to Old Windsor Lock. The lock keeper watched as I walked toward him, an angry look on his face. He very sternly asked what I was doing there. Hadn't I read the signs? I feebly replied that I thought it was an old sign. I told him where I was going, and asked him where to go from there. He softened somewhat and directed me to a bus stop, across and down the road, where I could take a bus to Staines, the next stop. I would not be able to follow the Path, but could pick it up again at Staines.

I hated to skip some of the trail--perhaps two miles, I estimated--but I had no choice. I admit to feeling sheepish--nay, guilty--over ignoring the sign, knowing how serious my misdemeanor could have been.

My unexpected bus detour led me away from two memorials not far off the Path: Magna Carta Island, where the Great Charter was reputedly signed in 1215, and the John F. Kennedy memorial. As well, I would like to have seen the "coalpost" by the towpath, one of many white, iron posts that surrounded the entries to London under an act of 1831, to remind merchants that a levy on coal was due. And further along, at Chertsey Meads, I would have seen, for the last time, a Thames water meadow scene.

The Staines bus station backed up against High Street. I ate my lunch in a big shopping center there, withdrew money from an ATM, and made a few phone calls to reserve a room in Shepperton, my next overnight stop.

It was threatening rain as I was preparing to leave Staines. I pulled on my rain gear and off I went, ready for the next adventure. After asking for directions from anyone I felt I could approach, I was soon back on the Path. I crossed over an open grass area, onto a gravel track, and came to Penton Hook Lock. The guidebook describes the Hook as, "surely the most impressive river loop along the Thames." It was well worth the time crossing the Penton lock to briefly explore tree-covered Penton Hook Island--very natural in feeling and appearance.

About one and a half miles from Shepperton, past Chertsey Lock, another sign announced that the Path was closed here, too, due to hoof and mouth disease. This time, I stopped at a pub--the Kingfisher in Chertsey--for information. It was easily the most beautiful pub I have seen. Its rich-looking, dark wood panels, wooden bar, wooden tables and chairs seemed like part of a luxurious hotel. The bartender was very helpful and took time to give me directions to Shepperton. He assured me that there was a sidewalk along the busy one-mile road. I was a little skeptical, but it turned out as he had said. In spite of the cold wind, it was an easy walk.

When I reached Shepperton, I stopped at a pub to pick up a salad for dinner. I did much better with food that day--no sugar, no white flour. My breakfast was fresh figs, strawberries and bananas with a muesli-type salad and yogurt, plus the usual Vega and orange juice. Yummy.

That night at 8:04, I was writing in my journal in bed because it was so cold in my room. I'd been warmer walking in the cold wind that afternoon than I was sitting in my room that evening. Christina, the B&B owner, a dear lady over sixty-five, was running the B&B for extra income to supplement her small £400-a-month pension. I presumed she couldn't afford to pay for heat. I took a hot shower and didn't complain about the cold because I felt sorry for her. And although Christina's place was a mile off the Path, I was grateful for a place to stay; the hotels were full that night.

I continued to be in good spirits, but as I got closer to London, I became more apprehensive about finding my way around the city.

DAY 13 SHEPPERTON - TEDDINGTON

Although my room last night was very cold, my bed was blessedly warm and cosy. Christina, my hostess, sat with me while we chatted over breakfast. When she thought of some additional fruit she could offer, she would get up and fetch it from the pantry or the garden. Breakfast was very wholesome and tasty--fresh raspberries, grapes and pears from her garden, muesli, and my regular Vega with orange juice. Delicious as it was, I could barely keep my mind off the cold and stop myself from shaking in her freezing kitchen.

I was relieved to get back outside, where the day was beginning to warm up. On the way through town, I found bananas for sale; I had been wanting to buy some for days. At the post office, I mailed home more papers and guidebook pages--120 grams, for a total now mailed of 220 grams, half a pound off the weight I had been carrying. Every ounce counts; it quickly adds up.

As I walked through Shepperton, I wondered how difficult it would be to find the Thames Path again, for I had arrived via the highway. Perhaps if I just headed for the river, there would be signs to direct me. There were, and I was pleased to find the Path easily. I chose to view that as a good omen for the day. It was now nine-thirty, and I had an eleven-mile walk to Teddington.

My guidebook indicated a choice of two routes. The ferry route followed the main river channel to Walton Bridge, while the alternate route went along the north bank river loop. A sign at the ferry point announced that the ferry was not running, so the choice was made for me. The route on the stream proved to be every bit as picturesque as the main river, and every bit as varied--trees, open grass areas, a gravel path, a wooden causeway, and a footbridge.

Not far beyond was Sunbury Weir, a favorite spot for freestyle kayaking, and beyond it, the original lock house, with the year "1812" inscribed on it. Today, the two Sunbury Locks are situated side by side further downstream. One, originally built in 1812, is hand-operated, but seldom used now; the other opened in 1927.

Further along, I passed between great concrete blocks that had been used in London's war defense.

Soon, the tower of Hampton Church, built in 1831, could be seen, and at a distance, the restored little temple that Shakespearean actor David Garrick had built to honor his Muse. On this side of the river, Canada Geese, pigeons, and ducks were taking advantage of a swan-feeding area.

Beyond several islands, the Path took me across a bridge to the north bank and over a pedestrian crossing to the gates of Hampton Court. The next stretch of the towpath, called Barge Walk, provided good views of the palace. Outside the fence, I walked by the long drive, the residence, the Banqueting House from World War II, and the south wing, then a large semicircle of formal gardens. I didn't linger. Compared to

Windsor Castle, Hampton Court appeared cheerless and uninviting. It lacks the setting and lovely gardens of Windsor, and to my untrained eye, its architecture appeared plain by English standards.

Soon Kingston Bridge appeared. As I left the Path and found my way into the town of Kingston, I was vigilant in noting my route so it would be easy for me to return to the Path later. I looked for a phone to reserve accommodation for the following night in Teddington.

The bright red telephone booths in England, now slowly disappearing, have become a British icon. Along Old London Road in Kingston lies a sculpture by David Mach entitled "Out of Order." It consists of twelve telephone boxes tipped to lean against one another like dominoes. It seems that the landmark sculpture is the subject of controversy; some love it, while others want it removed. I was neutral.

Kingston was occupied at one time by the Romans, and Saxon kings were crowned there. In 1965, it became a part of greater London and is now a university town. Kingston's ancient markets are still held daily in The Market Place, selling not only local produce, but also exotic foods, fish, flowers, and even jewelry. I was thrilled to find fresh figs in season at an astonishingly low price (under $2 Canadian per kilo). I lunched on them and some equally inexpensive avocados. I was tempted to buy some to take with me, but reminded myself that they would increase my load.

On my way back to the Path, I asked for directions to confirm that I was headed in the right direction. I get turned around so easily; I don't always trust my instincts.

The Path led under a railway bridge and on through the welcome greenery of tree-lined Canbury Gardens, fourteen and a half acres of award-winning park. I crossed a road and took a raised pathway. At the Half-Mile Tree, a local landmark, it is estimated that an elm tree (now replaced by a horse chestnut) once stood for more than five hundred years. Here the towpath begins again.

Across the river, the long Teddington weir begins, leading to a footbridge crossing over the river to Teddington. Although I didn't realize it at the time, Teddington is actually a largely suburban town in the Greater London borough of Richmond. It may have been the first permanent settlement in Saxon times. By the fourteenth century, it had a population of one to two hundred. Teddington is the site of the last lock on the river, and the beginning of the tidal Thames.

I was happy to have found accommodation in Teddington with my first call from Kingston. However, Linda, the B&B owner and I had had difficulty communicating. At the time, she was on a mobile phone away from her home, and we were repeatedly cut off. Finally, she was able to give me her address. I told her I would find her place and meet her there. I picked up a map at a real estate office in Teddington and went directly to her house. She wasn't home, but her next door neighbor saw me and offered to let me use her phone to call Linda. This time, we had a better connection, and she arrived home in five minutes.

There was delicious heat that night, and sole use of the bathroom across the hall. The room was very small, but clean and warm. Linda gave me directions to two pubs, the only eating establishments nearby. At The Antlers, I had a good green salad with sun-dried tomatoes, cooked mushrooms, and tasteless buffalo mozzarella cheese, which I later learned is actually made with water buffalo milk. "Gourmet" mixed greens were usually used in the pubs I had visited--no nutrition-less iceberg lettuce--and although I hadn't tried any high-priced restaurants to compare to, I got the best salads in pubs.

I was feeling more relaxed now about entering London proper and finding accommodation there. I had only the next night and Sunday night left to book.

DAY 14 TEDDINGTON - PUTNEY

At breakfast (fresh fruit, OJ with Vega and the best croissant I had ever tasted), I chatted with Linda, my hostess. I always had so many questions to ask about the area I was in and about England in general. Other than those actually walking it, she was the first person I met here who was knowledgeable about the Thames Path and what it was like to walk it.

It was rainy and windy most of the day. I kept my rain jacket hood up all afternoon and my waterproof gloves on all day. The rain made it more difficult to see the Path signs and read the guidebook, and to have a good look at the sights along the way, but other than that, the walking was fine.

The Path now followed both sides of the river. I opted to walk the South side, which was shorter; I was glad that I had, for it was very scenic. From the towpath at the Teddington footbridge, there was a panoramic view of the Teddington locks system: not just one lock, but a series--a skiff lock, a launch lock, and a barge lock.

The Path led into a rural area--the scrub and grasslands of Ham Lands, a natural reserve, home to a wide variety of birds, butterflies and plant species--and then it passed the landing steps for Hammerton's Ferry. The ferry provided a short ride across the river for pedestrians and cyclists.

Then came a view of Marble Hill, an exquisite little silver-white villa situated across the river in Marble Hill Park. The villa was built on sixty-six acres of riverside parkland near Richmond for Henrietta Howard, mistress of King George II when he was Prince of Wales. This place is said to exude an atmosphere of fashionable Georgian life.

Nearby is Petersham village, where explorer George Vancouver lived and is buried. At Petersham meadows, where cows still graze, the Path briefly left the riverside and soon came to Richmond. The stone arches of eighteenth-century Richmond Bridge and a waterfront development opened by the Queen in 1988 combine the old and the new. Not far away, traces remain of Henry VII's Richmond Palace.

Passing under bridges, the Path follows past Old Deer Park, an area of open space with a golf course and playing fields. Beyond Richmond Lock, the towpath is unusually wide, with the Thames on one side and a ditch of shrubs and other plants on the other.

Then, along Syon Reach, one can look across to a rare, preserved habitat: a tide meadow that is flooded twice a day. Upon arriving at Syon House, a grand manor house set in parklands and gardens, I found an open vista of Kew Gardens, three hundred acres of beauty and astonishing variety. Kew Palace, where royalty lived until 1818, was ahead. I would love to have visited the Gardens, but I knew that I would need at least a day to see even part of it.

So on I went, under the Kew Bridge and past Kew Pier, as I gazed at the inviting cottages of Strand on the Green across the river. Past Chiswick Bridge, I followed a bit of Mortlake riverside beneath the eight-story Mortlake brewery, which has been in existence since the fifteenth century. This solid block of a building is now a London landmark.

Just past Barnes Bridge railway station, the eighteenth and nineteenth century Georgian mansion villas of Barnes Terrace could be seen.

Past Hammersmith Bridge, another landmark--Harrod's Depository, with its familiar facade preserved--is now a residential estate, no longer owned by Harrod's.

Then I approached the open greenery of the Wetlands Center, where nearly forty acres of reservoir attracts some of the world's rarest waterbirds.

The rowing clubhouses I passed reminded me that this was the starting point for the Oxford and Cambridge Boat Race.

At the Putney waterfront, the towpath ended. I bid it a fond farewell. My long-ago dream of traveling it had come true. The dream was so different from the reality. In my dream, there were thatched English cottages standing alone by the towpath. Except for a few in the Cotswolds, the romantic cottages I had pictured, with their flower-filled gardens, were in villages. However, the lock keepers' houses came close to that vision. And I had pictured clear, uninterrupted path all along the river for miles and miles. At first, I'd been disappointed, but the reality soon surpassed my expectation.

Putney is a major center in Greater London, the most accessible of its suburbs. For centuries, Londoners went to Putney for leisure in the open spaces and clean air. The first permanent Putney Bridge between Putney and Fulham was built in 1729 to replace the ferry. In 1886, that bridge was torn down and the present stone structure built in its place.

As I entered Putney, it was raining heavily, and I had yet to find a place to stay. It was challenging to read the guidebook through my rain-covered glasses and the plastic-enclosed pages. There was no Tourist Information Center listed, nothing helpful at the train station, and although I got some leads at the library, I had no map and no idea where these places were. I called a Best Western; no one answered.

I had arrived early, around two p.m., at Putney Bridge. I could have kept going and looked for something further on, but for some unknown reason, I was reluctant. By the time I had crossed the rather long bridge twice, searching for places, it was four p.m. and the skies so overcast that it was already getting dark, and still raining heavily. I was discouraged and pessimistic.

Earlier, I had inquired about a room at a Travel Inn. There was one available for £79 (close to $200 CD), way over my budget. But standing there in the relentless rain, I resigned myself to paying the price. I returned to the Travel Inn and reserved a room--hard for me to accept.

Something strange about Putney--- Before leaving on the trip, I had tried to arrange accommodation there for this very night. Nothing came together and I eventually let it go, thinking I would find something when I arrived. And when I reached Putney, it didn't get any easier. It was so confusing trying to find my way around, looking for accommodation on both sides of the bridge and, at the same time, searching for a restaurant for dinner.

However, I had better luck when it came to dinner. I was pleased to find The Natural Cafe, a familiar name. I had eaten in one earlier on this trip and, like today, enjoyed a salad and dessert from the salad bar.

As I headed back to the Travel Inn after dinner, I realized with a start that I was now in suburban London. I thought, "So this is what London is like." The rush hour was just like every other city I've been in, only busier, with everyone intent on getting to their destination as fast as they could. I wouldn't describe it as frantic, but it surely was intense.

Over the whole trip, this day was my low point, emotionally. I was feeling out of sorts when I entered my hotel room. It may have had to do with the hectic street, the weather, or my reaction to the unwelcoming Putney main street. I stood in the middle of my spacious room and a wave of loneliness came over me (the only time on the trip). I soon brought myself out of the mood by focusing on all the positives, and giving thanks for Higher Guidance and assistance. I smiled at the contrast between this $200 room--with its heated towel bars, telephone and air conditioning/heating system--and some of the B&Bs I had stayed in. Four of the B&B rooms would have fit into this place (but no breakfast was included here). I settled in, did my usual evening chores--hand laundry, filling my water bladder, bringing my journal up to date, showering--watched a TV sitcom (a nice diversion), and went to bed in a peaceful state of mind.

DAY 15 PUTNEY - LONDON

Although I've read rave reviews about how great Putney is, I was happy to leave it this morning. It may have been the non-stop rain, the frustration of searching for a room when I could hardly see where I was going, or the sterility of the hotel room, but there was something about the place that made me glad my stay was over. Nevertheless, I would be interested in returning someday to see how I feel about it then.

Downstream from Putney Bridge, I joined the Path and followed it across a dock inlet, under a railway, and through the playing fields of Hurlington Park, onto a road, and back to the river.

Leaving Putney, the Path follows both sides of the river. Along today's section of the Thames, sixteen bridges provided opportunities to cross over to the opposite bank. It would take an entire book to describe the sights from Putney to London proper. I would love to do the walk again to explore the countryside and the countless visual delights along the way.

Most of today's walk was very different from the Path so far. Meadows and fields and villages were left behind, and palaces, office blocks, marinas and boulevards took their place.

After detouring around buildings, crossing bridges that led onto and off roads, past apartment blocks, through gates and past the open grass of a little park, I found my way to Imperial Wharf, a riverside complex of shops, apartments, a pub, waterfalls and planted beds on the site of a former industrial area.

Luxury cruisers were moored on the river along the cobbled walk of Chelsea Harbor. The Path kept more closely to the river now. It led up a tiled way to the unattractive walls of Lots Road Power Station, then bent right and left before reaching a terrace of charming Victorian cottages.

Today, only a tiny patch and the white gates remain of Cremorne Gardens, a pleasure destination around 1845-1877. During that period, from three p.m. until midnight, it was the scene of concerts, dancing, fireworks, balloon descents, equestrian exhibitions, and the endless creative offerings of its organizers. It is said that as many as two thousand people visited it nightly.

The Path led to Cheyne Walk, the site of a former riverside village that attracted many writers and artists--Whistler, Turner, George Elliott--and its most famous resident, Thomas More, who was beheaded in 1535 for opposing Henry VIII's religious reform. On some buildings, a blue plaque commemorates a famous personage who lived, worked, or visited there. Cheyne Walk lost its river frontage in 1870, when the Embankment was built upon land reclaimed from the foreshore.

The walkway passed under the pretty, but rather fragile-looking, Albert Bridge, a swing bridge built in the 1870s. Then some welcome greenery: the path goes by Chelsea Psychic Garden, the second oldest botanical garden in Britain.

Past Chelsea Bridge, at Nine Elms Reach, the solid, deserted-looking hulk of Battersea Power Station appeared. Originally a coal-fired station built in two stages in the 1930s and 1950s, it ceased operating in 1983 and has since become a London landmark. Since I was there in 2007, it has been developed into residential apartments.

I arrived at Vauxhall Bridge, a blue and red steel and granite-decked arch bridge between Pimlico and Vauxhall, opened in 1906. It has been placed on the Statutory List of Buildings of Special Architectural or Historic Interest, a widely used status applied to some half million structures in the United Kingdom.

I turned a corner and there they were--Jewel Tower, the Parliament Buildings and Westminster Abbey. Of this my guidebook says, "There is almost too much to view." What an impressive sight! I stared at these buildings; somehow, they didn't seem quite real. For so long, I have just heard about them, and seen photos and their images in the movies and on TV.

Jewel Tower is one of only two surviving sections of the medieval royal palace of Westminster, built in 1365-66 to house the treasures of Edward III. The three-story detached building has more recently been used to store historic records, and now contains exhibitions on the first two floors. It stands across the road from the current Palace of Westminster, home of the British Parliament.

As I approached the Houses of Parliament, and saw the long queues of people waiting for admission, I debated joining them, until I realized that the line wasn't moving, and wouldn't move until the opening at one p.m., almost another hour.

I stopped to gaze at Westminster Abbey to my left. With more than a thousand years of history, it is one of the most important Gothic buildings in the country. It has been the church for coronations since 1066, and seventeen monarchs are buried there. Henry III began the present church in 1245, and it currently contains stained glass, textiles, valued paintings and important archives.

Down the way, the Path passed beneath the clock tower housing the London icon, Big Ben. This nickname was given to the clock tower bell, which weighs more than thirteen tons. In 2012, the clock tower was renamed Elizabeth Tower, in honor of Queen Elizabeth II's Diamond Jubilee.

A few steps away, the Path carried on along the Victoria Embankment, which encloses London's main drainage system.

I soon came to Blackfriars Bridge, named after Blackfriars Monastery, which once stood nearby. As a much-needed supplement to London Bridge, it was originally built in 1769, and rebuilt in 1869. Stone carvings of water birds grace its piers. Near the bridge, signs direct one to Paul's Walk, the middle aisle of Old St. Paul's Cathedral, where people walked up and down in Elizabethan times in search of the latest news.

The path goes along the wharf, diverts to a service road beside the traffic of Upper Thames Street, and back and forth through gates to and from the riverside.

London Bridge, the first stone bridge in London, was erected in 1209, but there have been several others since. Until Putney Bridge opened in 1729, London Bridge was the only road-crossing of the Thames downstream of Kingston. The London Bridge of 1831 was bought by a U.S. magnate in 1968, taken down stone by stone, shipped and reassembled as a tourist attraction in Arizona, U.S.

Then I came to the Billingsgate Market building, restored in 1982 after its fish market closed. Along the riverside here, customs officers have checked goods due for duties since Elizabethan times. Custom House Quay is the next site on the Path.

The walkway goes along the river frontage to Tower Pier, and then to the Tower of London. Here I stepped off the Path and asked for directions to the nearest underground station. I had no idea how to proceed from there, but when I arrived, I was thrilled to discover how simple it was. All the signs and route maps made it easy to find which train to take to King's Cross, the station closest to St. Pancras Hostel, where I had booked a reservation for the night.

This would be my first experience staying in a hostel. I checked in at three p.m., and had a look around--clean, orderly, quiet--quite acceptable. Then, from the hostel, I sent e-mails to family and a friend.

I left for dinner before my three roommates arrived. The Pizza Express was nearby--a big restaurant of forty to fifty tables, and very noisy, due to low ceilings and lots of kids celebrating birthdays or something. The salad of greens with peas, broad beans and green beans in mustard dressing was quite tasty, as was the chocolate cake served on a large plate of heavy cream.

There I was in the heart of London, having walked to the Tower of London today--and only one day left on the Path! I was in great spirits. There was so much to see, and it was so helpful to have the guidebook identify the sights, and give interesting information about them. Tomorrow would be an entirely different day; I was looking forward to it.

A DAY OFF IN LONDON

Breakfast was served cafeteria-style at the YHA St. Pancras hostel near Regent Park--muesli, apple, croissant, and orange juice, with my added Vega.

At 8:45, I set off for morning service at the Self-Realization Fellowship London Center, about a half-hour away. Marylebone Street was almost deserted--not surprising at this hour on a Sunday morning. I had picked up a street map at the hostel, and as I walked along, I stopped now and then to check it for directions. At one intersection, a man advised me that it might not be wise to be seen on the street carrying an open map. I wasn't concerned, but decided it wouldn't hurt to be more discreet, so I folded up the map, leaving only the area of my present location quickly accessible. I found the Center without difficulty, and congratulated myself for taking the time before leaving on this trip to make the necessary preparations for attending--finding a hostel nearby and arranging to be in London on a Sunday.

After a lovely service, I left the Center and returned to the hostel to pick up my belongings, for I would be staying that night at a different hostel, closer to the Path. By now, it was well past noon and I was hungry. I wanted to have lunch in Soho.

Using the map as a guide, I shortly arrived in Soho District. For years, I had heard so much about Soho in books, movies and songs. I knew that it had been a popular place for intellectuals in the early 1900s, and later, in the 1950s, became a center for beatniks. I had an image of a trendy area, filled with delightful restaurants that served wonderful food served in innovative ways. It wasn't as I had expected. Yes, it had countless restaurants, and the streets were swarming with people, but it didn't seem to have the vibrancy and character I envisioned. Yet even today, it has been described as one of London's most exciting and unique centers. Aside from the restaurants, clubs, and late-night coffee shops, it has become a multicultural area, home to industry and commerce. Both rich and poor live there.

Some streets were closed off to vehicles due to the huge crowds in the streets on weekends. I wandered around, taking it all in as I searched for a restaurant with something different on the menu, lots of atmosphere and reasonable prices. I finally settled for a small Thai place with a wide variety of items in its vegetarian buffet. Overall, I would give it three and a half stars. It was good, but not great.

Piccadilly Circus was on my list to visit next. When I arrived there and viewed the crowds of pedestrians and the congestion of traffic coming from all directions, I thought, "Now I know why it's called a circus." It was fascinating to watch all the activity, but I thought there must be more to it than just an intersection. I didn't know that the word, 'circus,' in this context, is derived from a Latin word meaning 'circle,' a wide-open space at a street junction. This junction, built in 1819, connects Regent Street with the major shopping streets of Piccadilly.

I was standing on a street corner, once again looking at a map, when a woman, also with a map, came up beside me. She, too, was from Canada. I asked for directions to Trafalgar Square, but she advised me to first visit Covent Gardens. I hadn't intended to go there, but changed my mind.

Covent Gardens, a former fruit and vegetable market, is now a popular shopping and tourist site, with small shops, cafes and pubs. I didn't linger there; it was so crowded, I could barely move. And it didn't offer anything that I hadn't seen in similar markets in other countries.

Trafalgar Square, however, more than made up for my disappointments with Soho and Covent Gardens. The Square was much larger than I had imagined. There seemed to be a vibrancy, unlike some other open public places, where people seem preoccupied, or just intent on getting where they are going. The focal point of Trafalgar Square is, of course, the tall column topped with the statue of Admiral Horatio Nelson, who commanded the British fleet to victory against France and Spain at Trafalgar in 1805. The large open space of the Square is surrounded by three roads and a terrace leading to the famous National Gallery art museum. I wandered around the Square, enjoying its atmosphere.

Although the morning had been chilly, it was now a lovely, sunny day. I wanted to stay longer, but it was time to find my way back to the Thames and follow it to my next hostel. St. Paul's Hostel is older and more worn than St. Pancras, possibly because more tourists have trod its halls over the years. My private room had a sink, TV, heater, a window that opened (important for me), and a clean bed. The shared bathroom was next door. So far, so good.

DAY 16 TOWER BRIDGE – THAMES BARRIER

As I started out on the final leg of my journey, I was in a different state of mind than on the rest of my walk. My day off yesterday had broken my momentum and interrupted the rhythm of my days on the Path. Although today seemed anti-climactic, this did not lessen my desire to complete the walk--- it was something I definitely wanted to do.

I took the tube back to Tower Hill station and joined the Path at 9:25 a.m. Past the visitors' shop to the cabled Tower Wharf, by Traitor's Gate to Tower Bridge, I went. The distinguished shape of Tower Bridge was easily discernible through the rain. Its unique design, I learned, was created to allow tall ships to pass through, a rare occurrence now. Of the many bridges I have seen and crossed on this journey, Tower Bridge is, to me, one of the most impressive. It is so British, and so appropriate for London.

I crossed under the Bridge. It was pouring rain, and it continued to rain most of the day. This didn't deter me. I was cosy in my comfortable rain gear, and excited about the prospect of reaching my goal. The unfortunate part was that I couldn't get a good view of many sights along the way, and I couldn't read my guidebook to identify what I was able to see.

From Tower Bridge, the Thames Path National Trail follows both sides of the river as far as the Isle of Dogs. From there, the Path continues on the south bank only. Since I had opted to travel on the north bank, I would have to cross over to the south side at the Isle of Dogs, and then follow the Path to the Thames Barrier, the end of my journey.

Soon after I left Tower Bridge, I stopped to admire the bronze water sculpture, Girl with a Dolphin, by David Wynne, and later I came to the Dickens Inn, a former brewery, now restyled and reconstructed near the entry to St. Katherine Docks. These docks, now sporting a marina, shops, bars, restaurants and a housing and leisure complex, have been a focus of commerce and other enterprises since the tenth century. It was one of the areas of the Docklands badly damaged by German bombing in World War II.

The Path followed the riverside as much as possible, frequently going around the remaining warehouses from one wharf to another. There were stretches that had been changed from predominantly industrial to mainly residential, with a mix of converted warehouses and new apartment buildings.

The section of the walk from Tower Bridge to Greenwich abounded with superb views and impressive historical sites on both sides of the river. The docks were the scene of wide trade with the world in the early days, when the Port of London was the world's busiest port. New shipping practices and the docks' inability to accommodate very large ships were instrumental in contributing to their decline. They were closed between 1960 and 1980, leaving about eight square miles of derelict land, poverty, and unemployment. Revival of the area, now known as the Docklands, began in the 1970-1980s.

Along Wapping High Street, the Path led to the Waterside Gardens at Wapping New Stairs. It is said that this may have been the site of Execution Dock, where pirates, such as Captain Kid, were executed.

Near Shadwell Basin, The Prospect of Whitby pub offered a picturesque point for Whistler and Turner to paint some of their famous riverside scenes. It was also a favorite drinking place for Charles Dickens and Samuel Pepys.

Along a bend in the river at the Isle of Dogs, the iconic skyline of Canary Wharf, with its striking architecture, could be seen. Clipper ships regularly use the pier here. This is one of London's major financial centers, also known for its exclusive shops and restaurants. The stainless steel fifty-story skyscraper here--One Canada Square, the second tallest building in Britain--is a prestigious location for offices.

The Path on this side of the river ended at Island Gardens. Ahead a sign--"Thames Path Greenwich quarter mile"-- announced the Greenwich Foot Tunnel. This is the point where the Thames Path leaves the north bank and follows the south bank only. I opted to take the stairs rather than the lift down into the tunnel, which is fifty-three feet under the Thames at high tide and thirty-three feet at low tide. I believe it was low tide at the time, but what did it matter?

At the bottom of the hundred stairs, the tunnel floor slopes down, then levels out for a while before climbing once again. I walked quickly along through the stark, cool and dark cavern, reminding myself that it was only a quarter-mile long. Someone described this walk as an "unnerving, intimidating experience." I certainly felt alone and cut off from the rest of the world. Nevertheless, I wasn't regretting my choice. I knew when I chose to take the north path that I would have to go through the tunnel to join the south Path.

Every time fear is faced and overcome, it is a victory. Would I walk through the tunnel again? Yes, if I thought it was necessary. Would I choose to do it again? No. However, it was an easier thing for me to do than ride a roller coaster, for example, or walk on a long swinging bridge across a deep canyon.

Perhaps the reader would be interested now in some of the sights to be found on the south side of the river--the side I had not chosen to walk-- before Greenwich.

Past the King's Stairs, there is the Mayflower pub, named after the famous ship that began its epic journey from here, carrying the Pilgrim Fathers to America in 1620. The pub displays the Mayflower passenger list and the Last Will and Testament of the ships' crew. Four of the Mayflower's owners are buried in St. Mary's Church, across the road.

The Surrey Docks Farm, at the site of the eighteenth-century shipyard, is 2.2 acres of working farm, providing education for the public. It has a variety of animals, some live, and some in the form of bronze statues.

At Deptford Creek, where the River Ravensbourne enters the Thames, there is a statue of Peter the Great. The statue was erected in 2001 to commemorate his visit to England in the seventeenth century to study new developments in technology, particularly shipbuilding.

A nearby landmark is the Cutty Sark, one of the fastest sailing ships of her day and the last tea-clipper built. The ship was undergoing conservation in May, 2007, when it was badly damaged by fire. It has since been restored and was reopened to the public in 2012.

I exited the tunnel and continued on the Path along the river frontage to Greenwich University, formerly Royal Naval College. In the background, just before the University, is Queen's House, a former palace, but now part of the National Maritime Museum. As a backdrop, on a hill in Greenwich Park overlooking the Thames, stands the Royal Observatory, London's only planetarium. Home of Greenwich Mean Time, it is situated at zero degrees longitude, and marks the Prime Meridian line. The line, which runs through the courtyard, was at one time marked with a brass strip, later changed to stainless steel. Since 1999, it can be seen at night as a powerful green laser shining north across the sky.

From here, the riverside is a mix of warehouses, wharves, slipways, abandoned buildings, and converted flats. Information boards along the way relate the history of the wharves.

Then I reached the Millennium Dome in the Docklands region. This dome-shaped structure was initially built to house an exhibition for the approach of the third millennium, but attendance receipts couldn't cover the enormous building and maintenance costs. In 2007, it was renovated and reopened as O2 Arena, now a popular concert venue. In 2012, it provided a site for the London Olympic Games.

I circled the Arena and continued on, attempting unsuccessfully to read my guidebook through my rain-covered eyeglasses and the plastic-enclosed guidebook pages. And in those rare instances when I could read the guidebook, I couldn't understand its directions. At times, even the river couldn't be used as a landmark, because the Path moved away from it. As a result, I wasn't sure where I was. I walked for miles and miles and finally admitted I was lost. I asked many people for directions--some were helpful, some not. For long stretches, there was no one around to ask, absolutely no one in sight. I was determined not to get upset, to stay calm, and remember that I had always been guided before and I would be guided now. To this day, I don't know where I went or how I could have gotten so lost.

After it seemed like I had walked for miles in desolated areas, I turned around and somehow found my way back to the Millennium Dome, a point where the river and the Path made a sharp right turn. I again asked for directions and proceeded in the direction indicated. I plodded on, and finally, to my great relief and delight, there they were--the ten stainless steel hoods of the Thames Barrier, sitting at the mouth of the Thames estuary--the place I had travelled over two hundred miles to reach.

Through the ten shipping gates that open and close as needed, the Barrier provides protection from flooding. In 1928, fourteen people died when the Thames flooded; and the North Sea flood of 1953, in which 307 died, caused much damage. It is estimated that after 2030, rising sea levels and tilting land will make the present barrier less effective.

Thrilled that I had found it at last, I completed the last few steps up and down and under the Barrier control center, eagerly anticipating a celebratory meal at the Barrier Buffet. To my dismay, but not my total surprise, I was told it was closed because of some debris that had washed into the Barrier turbines. Sticking to my determination to remain unruffled, I asked for directions to another restaurant. Fortunately, it was close and easy to find, but it was closing shortly and had little food left. Still undeterred, I ordered a package of hot chocolate and one of scones and quickly consumed them. What an anticlimactic, inglorious conclusion to my walk!

Back at the Millennium Dome, I got on the tube and made one transfer, without any mishaps, to St. Paul's Hostel. However, and I'm feeling embarrassed about admitting this, it took much trial and error before I could locate Carter Lane, the site of the hostel--even with a map. In my defense, I'm going to say that it is a short one-block lane, not easy to find, even when I basically knew where it was.

My walk today had taken much longer than I had anticipated, almost six hours to walk ten miles.

I was in good spirits as I again left the hostel around 6:30 to pick up some sushi from a shop, fortunately just around the corner. I was content as I ate my dinner in the lounge while conversing with a woman from Australia (in London for the fifth time and planning to spend a year here), a man from England who stayed in the hostel during his workweek and went home on weekends, an American woman, and a male Argentinian couple from north of Los Angeles, California. There were varying perspectives on British political and economic issues, and good suggestions for things to see and do in London. A lovely ending to a triumphant day.

LONDON

I had two days left to spend in London before flying home from Gatwick.

My room last night was acceptable, a five-bed dorm with a sink in the room and windows that could be opened. I appreciated the consideration of my roommates, who quietly settled in when they arrived during the night.

In the morning, I went on a tour of the Tower of London. The "Tower," as it is known, is a complex of several buildings enclosed within two concentric walls and a moat. Although the Beefeater guide was very much into the gory aspects of the Tower, he gave an interesting history of the place.

William the Conquerer built this as a fortress, making some of the walls fifteen feet thick. The tower and moat and other structures, such as the mint, were added later. Much of the stone came from France. Later, the "Tower" became a refuge for the monarchs, providing easy access to the nearby Thames.

After the one-hour tour, we were left to explore on our own.

William built the plain white structure on the site for himself as a royal palace. The kings and queens kept their exotic beasts here (Henry III had a polar bear) and also their valuable jewelry and accoutrements. I stopped to see the crown jewels. To someone who is knowledgeable about jewels, this may have held some fascination, but I had no more than a curiosity about them.

The Tower of London is perhaps most famous as a notorious prison and place of torture and execution. With a shudder, I skipped the infamous Bloody Tower, where people were once beheaded, and I avoided the display of methods of torture, but enjoyed the armor display in the artillery room.

I left Tower Hill thinking about the times of William the Conquerer. It seemed that, for most, life was so short and precarious then, with little opportunity for improvement.

I had planned to go to St. Paul's Cathedral that afternoon, but unfortunately, it was closed. I decided to cancel my plans to visit Buckingham Palace and Harrods the next morning and go to St. Paul's Cathedral then instead.

That afternoon, I settled into a sofa in the hostel lounge with a newspaper and my journal. It was raining; I had had eighteen non-stop days on the go. All I wanted to do was relax.

Before breakfast the next morning, I caught up on my journal-writing in the hostel laundry room while waiting for my laundry to dry. What a pleasure to have laundry facilities once again! I sat at breakfast with a very amiable young Englishman, who was staying in the hostel until he could move into his recently purchased £120,000 flat, the least expensive flat on the ground floor of a very modest building. He was very helpful in telling me about places to visit and how to get there. Our conversation turned to the lack of a Canadian presence in

England, in terms of how little Canada is mentioned or its influence felt as compared to the huge awareness of Australia and the U.S.

St. Paul's Cathedral sits at the top of Ludgate Hill, the highest point in the city of London. Its famous dome is a symbol of London, its heritage and its spiritual life. It is an important meeting place, a center for the arts, and for learning and public debate. It has been the scene of many special ceremonies: funeral services for Nelson, Winston Churchill, and Margaret Thatcher; the wedding of Charles, Prince of Wales and Lady Diane Spencer; the celebration of the eightieth birthday and Diamond Jubilee of Elizabeth II.

It is believed that the original St. Paul's church, founded in 604 AD, may have been built on this site; others replaced it. The present St. Paul's, designed by Sir Christopher Wren, was completed in 1711 as part of a major rebuilding plan after the Great Fire of London in 1666.

St. Paul's Cathedral was so overwhelmingly beautiful, I couldn't take it all in. I made my way around the cathedral and often just stood there, awe-struck at the marvelous architecture. I was about to start the ascent of over four hundred steps to the top gallery when I realized that it wouldn't be wise to attempt the steep climb carrying my full pack on my back. So I turned and left with very mixed feelings. Although I had already seen more than I could absorb--it is artistically magnificent beyond description--it would be great to view it, and London, from the galleries. I went for lunch to think it over.

I chose a nearby tea shop called "Tea," which served good quality food. After soup and a brownie, I had to satisfy my curiosity and try their flapjacks. In Canada, a flapjack is a pancake served with butter, syrup, and sometimes bacon. Here, it was like a chewy cookie made mainly from oatmeal, brown sugar, butter and raisins--quite tasty.

Over lunch, I decided to return to the hostel I had already checked out of, and get permission to store my backpack in a locker in their luggage room. I accomplished that without difficulty and returned unencumbered to the Cathedral.

Up the 437 steps I climbed in the narrow, circular staircases, stopping at all three galleries for the view. The first, the Whispering Gallery, overlooks the altar, organ, and nave on the floor far below. I experimented with other people, and was able to hear their whispered sounds from the opposite side of the gallery. This phenomenon can sometimes be present in caves, and has been detected in other famous buildings, such as the Temple of Heaven in Beijing.

The next gallery, on the outside of the building, was built around a stone dome. Walking around it, I peered through the stone columns at the city below. Another 152 steps, and I reached the Golden Gallery. I slowly walked along the iron rail for a 360-degree view far above the city of London. Cloud and smog partially hid distant parts of the city. Somehow, London from above seemed more familiar, as if it could be any city that I knew. Yet I kept saying to myself, "This is London below. Imagine that! I am able to stand here and see the whole city."

I went below to the Crypt to find some of the tombs I hadn't seen before lunch--among them that of Lord Wellington, Lord Nelson (whose casket was made from the wood of a French ship he had defeated in battle), and Sir Christopher Wren (whose epitaph was written in Latin by his son and read, "Reader, if you seek his monument, look around you."). I was surprised to discover that one area of the Crypt has a huge unique space used for events, such as a sit-down dinner for up to 250 guests.

Certainly, the Cathedral was one of the highlights of my trip (and a stark contrast to the Tower of London). Sir Christopher Wren must have had direct inspiration from the heavenly realms when he designed St. Paul's.

I needn't have worried about finding my way around London. London is a sightseer's dream for one who likes to walk. So many of the major sights are within a mile radius, and others are easily accessible in less than a day. My time in London was a fitting ending to my trip, for it compensated, to a degree, for all the sights along the way that I didn't have the time to explore and enjoy.

EPILOGUE

The Thames Path was so much more for me than just a solo hike along a river in a new country. It wasn't just a two-hundred-mile walk, but a journey of getting to know myself, of discovering my strengths and weaknesses, and becoming aware of my degree of tolerance for things and circumstances that didn't quite please me, and even made me fearful. Normally, in daily life, I am okay with being alone. This has not been a challenge for me. But being alone in a strange country calls upon a greater degree of fearlessness, of courage, and willingness to accept the unexpected. It forced me mentally, physically, and spiritually to step out of my comfort zone.

Spiritually, the experience tested me, and ultimately strengthened my faith in God. As I became more aware of the ever-changing ups and downs of my mental state, I set a goal to stay even-minded through the challenges and the high points, a goal that I didn't reach until the last day of my walk. I even began to give thanks for all the opportunities to learn from my mishaps and the numerous times things didn't work out as expected. Today, I am more confident of my abilities. I am more able to stay in the day, and not worry about tomorrow.

This was an adventure. When I left home, I was a clean slate, ready to be written on. It seemed like every moment was an experience never before seen, nor felt exactly like this. I immersed myself in it. I thrilled to all the new sights and smells--even the air was different from what I had experienced anywhere else. It was an enriching experience, learning about the history, culture, and people of another land.

I felt at home in all of England--I was very comfortable there. But it was the Cotswolds, in particular, that made my heart skip a beat. The picturesque stone cottages of its villages, the meandering stream of the Thames, the meadows and fields evoked feelings of peace and contentment. To this day, that area stands out most vividly in my memory and fills me with a longing to return.

I loved the simplicity of my life during the three weeks. There was nothing else I needed to be doing. I had everything I needed; I was self-contained. I was free.

The biggest factor in my success was my mindset--my faith in Spirit, my belief that I could do it, my willingness to take risks and, perhaps most of all, my strong desire to succeed. My love of walking helped. My innate curiosity and my desire for adventure propelled me forward each day.

Following the Path was, for me, a series of sixteen walks, rather than one walk of sixteen days. Each day had its destination, its plan, and its goal. Each day was unique, independent of any other. Consequently, when I reached the Thames Barrier on that last day, it felt, in a sense, like just another day completed. The victory lay in doing what I set out to do each day; accepting with trust, whatever I encountered. The journey was the thing.

APPENDIX

MY PACKING LIST

BACKPACK — Expensive, but worth every penny. Sized to fit my torso length, with eight sets of adjustable straps, an air space at the back, and designed to hold a water bladder with a feed tube.

WATER BLADDER

BACKPACK RAIN COVER

SILK ENVELOPE BED SHEET — (I never used it.)

HAND TOWELS — Small, absorbent, quick drying.

TWO PAIRS LONG PANTS — Could become capris or shorts by unzipping hidden zippers.

ONE SHORT-SLEEVED TOP

TWO LONG-SLEEVED TOPS — Designed to wick moisture away from the skin.

WINDBREAKER JACKET

WATERPROOF PANTS AND RAIN JACKET WITH HOOD

WATERPROOF GLOVES

UNDERWEAR AND SOCKS — Fast-drying.

HIKING BOOTS — Waterproof. (Many boots are water repellant; it was much harder to find truly waterproof boots.)

MISCELLANEOUS — Air ticket and accommodation reservations, cash, credit cards, flashlight, lock for locker, two guidebooks, London map, GPS (never used), two batteries, journal and pen, personal items, moleskin, and band-aids.

FOOD — Energy bars, fruit leather, ground nuts, nori sheets, dried fruit, Vega smoothie supplement, Cell Food, maca, and chlorella supplements.

BIBLIOGRAPHY

Acroyd, Peter. Thames, the Biography. Anchor Books, 2009.

Schneer, Jonathan. The Thames. Little, Brown, and Company, 2005.

Sharp, David. The Thames Path. National Trail Guides. Aurum Press in association with Natural England and The Ramblers' Association, 2007.

Weightman, Gavin. London's Thames, The River That Shaped a City and Its History. John Murray, publishers, 2005.

Printed in Great Britain
by Amazon

52784939R00067